24,50

MILL ON BENTHAM AND COLERIDGE

MILL ON BENTHAM
AND COLERIDGE

**WITH
AN INTRODUCTION BY**

F. R. Leavis

CAMBRIDGE UNIVERSITY PRESS

Cambridge
London   New York   New Rochelle
Melbourne   Sydney

Published by the Press Syndicate of the University of Cambridge
The Pitt Building, Trumpington Street, Cambridge CB2 1RP
32 East 57th Street, New York, NY 10022, USA
296 Beaconsfield Parade, Middle Park, Melbourne 3206, Australia

Introduction copyright 1950 by F. R. Leavis; copyright 1978 by Mrs Q. D. Lea

First published by Chatto & Windus 1950
First published by the Cambridge University Press 1980

Printed in the United States of America
First printed in Great Britain by Butler and Tanner Ltd., Frome and London
Reprinted by Hamilton Printing Company, Rensselaer, NY

British Library Cataloguing in Publication Data

Mill, John Stuart
Mill on Bentham and Coleridge
1. Bentham, Jeremy
2. Coleridge, Samuel Taylor–Philosophy
I. Leavis, Frank Raymond
192   B1574.B34   79-42833

ISBN 0 521 23330 5 hard covers
ISBN 0 521 29917 9 paperback

CONTENTS

This present volume represents an ambition to make Mill's *Bentham* and *Coleridge* current classics for the literary student. But there was more to the actual operative purpose that moved me than this suggests, and 'for the literary student' doesn't, without some explaining, really convey my intention. And in the explaining I have to avow that, essentially, I have been concerned to take a propagandist opportunity. I have been concerned to do something more by way of promoting that particular approach to the problem of liberal education which I outlined in *Education and the University*. I contend there that while, on the one hand, if the study of literature is to play its central part it must be informed and governed by a more athletic conception of criticism as a discipline of intelligence than it commonly is, on the other a serious study of literature inevitably leads outwards into other studies and disciplines, into fields not primarily literary, and that the problem of liberal education at the university level, particular discipline being duly provided for, is to exploit this outward-leading to the best advantage. A liberal education cannot confine itself to the critical study of literature, and the profit of a real literary training will show itself very largely in other-than-literary fields. It is with the means of cultivating and relating these fields that a serious attempt to grapple with the problem must be very largely preoccupied.

This insistence on extra-literary studies may seem superfluous, the need being recognized in time-honoured and universal academic practice. My point is that my preoccupation with vindicating the study of literature as—what it so rarely is—a real discipline (and one without which there can be no real liberal education) carries with it, in the nature of things, a more exacting preoccupation with extra-literary studies than academic practice anywhere bears witness to. In the English Tripos, for instance, with which my own work has been associated, the 'period' papers which the candidate has to take are headed *Literature, Life and Thought*. But no one should suppose from this that candidates for the English Tripos will have been guided through courses of work planned in the interests of an extended and unified understanding of any period or any part of it—or anything at all. It means merely that, if an odd candidate, in picking, after a study of back papers, the minimum safe number of topics on which to acquire so much knowledge as will show to advantage in a half-hour's to an hour's unloading, decides in favour of one coming under 'Life and Thought', he can count, if he is judicious and moderately lucky, on finding his opportunity. It will be a very unusual and fortunate student who has the grasp, the energy and the character to make it anything else. Most will not even glimpse what else it might and should be.

And if we ask how anything better is to be arrived at, the answer is that nothing substantially better can, under a system that for guidance leaves the student, for the most part, to lectures, and reckons to test his quality by an end-of-course stand-and-deliver against the clock. Study under such a system inevitably tends to be an acquiring and arranging of cliché-material. The academic authorities believing in such a system will tend to take as their first-class man a type that may be described as the complete walking cliché—the man (it's often a woman) who unloads with such confident and accomplished ease in the examination-room because he has never really grappled with anything, and is uninhibited by any inkling of the difference between the retailing of his amassed externalities and the effort to think something out into a grasped and unified order that he has made his own. Those who like this type will recruit themselves from it, and will inevitably tend to dislike, and to undervalue as a student, the man who makes them uncomfortable by implicitly challenging their standards, their competence and their self-esteem: the system is disastrous and self-perpetuating. So the 'academic mind' comes to deserve its depressing reputation.

I have suggested in *Education and the University* what, in an 'English School' that is really designed to promote the development of mature, energetic and creative minds, will replace the reliance on lectures and examinations. I am not proposing to recapitulate here my account of the methods of study-group, organized discussion and 'pieces of work' that seem to me, in their general lines, necessary conditions of any promising attack on the problem. But—and that is why I refer to my account of them—assumed by me as the right or ideal conditions, they are there as an implicit context in the suggestions I make below. Not that I think that except where these ideal conditions obtain nothing is worth attempting. Opportunities far from ideal are worth making the most of, and it is out of experience of such that my suggestions come. Whenever, for instance (it is a good one for demonstrative purposes), one is faced with directing, as part of a much wider 'English' course, a study of the Victorian age, one can profitably ask oneself how such a study can be best approached and best organized. What are the likeliest lines for promoting, not the usual ready and confident superficiality of the 'good student', but that conscious and intelligent incompleteness which carries with it the principle of growth; not the canny amassing of inert material for the examination-room, but the organization that represents a measure of real understanding, and seeks of its very nature to extend and complete itself?

The opportunity I was endeavouring to make the most of when I thought of these two essays of Mill's, and of the reasons for making them more accessible, was a paper on George Eliot and her setting instituted for Part II of the English Tripos. A paper for Part II, the student being relatively mature, with a good deal of reading behind him, and some measure of real study in the given field being presumably expected by the examiners, affords a better opportunity than any 'Life and Thought' licence in Part I—opportunity for experiment that may nevertheless have bearings on work in less favourable conditions. 'Setting', presumably, meant something more than the immediate intellectual and cultural environment as given in the books on George Eliot; an environment that, if it is to be worth serious study, must be related to a much wider context: in fact, we seemed committed to a pretty general study of the Victorian background and (to change the metaphor) to attempting some sort of charting of the main currents.

In helping students to tackle such an enterprise one looks for the approach that promises to educe most readily the lines of significant organization—the main lines on which most things in the whole complex field can be most significantly related. Such help is peculiarly necessary where the Victorian age is concerned. The student is very unlikely to have brought any very useful notions of how to proceed from his earlier literary studies. A man who has taken Part I of the English Tripos will know something of Carlyle, Ruskin, Arnold, Newman, Macaulay and other representative figures, but (and this seems to me a damning comment on the system) unless he is very exceptional he will not know how to push further in pursuit of an ordered understanding without a prohibitive waste of time and energy. And—as, in my experience, the keenest and most competent searchers have verified—you may go through (say) Oliver Elton's *Survey of English Literature 1830–1880* without acquiring any better notion of how to deepen, extend and organize into real knowledge and understanding your smatterings and adumbrations.

It isn't, then, very helpful to suggest to your students that they should for a start, with the help of Elton's *Survey* and Trevelyan's *British History in the Nineteenth Century*, sketch a rough chart of the field, marking the main features and outlining the main currents. They need more specific suggestions if they are to get their bearings in the age and establish their axes of reference. And surely the first obvious suggestion is that, of all the Victorian figures they are already acquainted with, Matthew Arnold, because of the peculiar quality of his intelligence and the peculiar nature of his relation to his time, will repay special study in a way no others will; a suggestion to which the extremely useful book on him by Mr. Lionel Trilling,[1] lying to hand, gives the greater force. But something further is needed, a complementary focal line, and here it is that Mill presents himself as meeting the case ideally.

In the first place, of course, it is his 'Bentham' and

[1] *Matthew Arnold*, by Lionel Trilling (Allen & Unwin).

his 'Coleridge' that propose themselves: once they are thought of, their due status as key documents is indisputable. To begin with, the two subjects are the key figures that Mill so convincingly exhibits them as being. The essays are devoted to justifying the attribution of significance that he makes in the earlier of them, that on Bentham (1838):

'There are two men, recently deceased, to whom their country is indebted not only for the greater part of the important ideas which have been thrown into circulation among its thinking men in their time, but for a revolution in its general modes of thought and investigation . . . The writers of whom we speak have never been read by the multitude; except for the more slight of their works, their readers have been few: but they have been the teachers of the teachers; there is hardly to be found in England an individual of any importance in the world of mind, who (whatever opinions he may have afterwards adopted) did not first learn to think from one of these two; and though their influences have but begun to diffuse themselves through these intermediate channels over society at large, there is already scarcely a publication of any consequence addressed to the educated classes, which, if these persons had not existed, would not have been different from what it is. These men are, Jeremy Bentham and Samuel Taylor Coleridge —the two great seminal minds of England in their age.'

But Bentham and Coleridge are not only, in actual history, the key and complementary powers by reference to which we can organize into significance so much of the field to be charted; even if they had had no great influence they would still have been the classical examples they are of two great opposing types of mind:

'It is hardly possible to speak of Coleridge, and his position among his contemporaries, without reverting to Bentham: they are connected by two of the closest bonds of association—resemblance and contrast. It would be difficult to find two persons of philosophic eminence more exactly the contrary of one another. Compare their modes of treatment of any subject, and you might fancy them inhabitants of different worlds. They seem to have scarcely a principle or a premise in common. Each of them sees scarcely anything but what the other does not see. Bentham would have regarded Coleridge with a peculiar measure of the good-humoured contempt with which he was accustomed to regard all modes of philosophizing different from his own. Coleridge would probably have made Bentham one of the exceptions to the enlarged and liberal appreciation which (to the credit of *his* mode of philosophizing) he extended to most thinkers of any eminence, from whom he differed.'

And as we follow Mill's analysis, exposition and evaluation of this pair of opposites we are at the same time, we realize, forming a close acquaintance with a mind different from either—the mind that appreciates both and sees them as both necessary, generalizing the necessity in these terms:

'For among the truths long recognized by Continental philosophers, but which very few Englishmen have yet arrived at, one is, the importance, in the present imperfect state of mental and social science, of antagonistic modes of thought: which, it will one day be felt, are as necessary to one another in speculation, as mutually checking powers are in a political constitution. A clear insight, indeed, into this necessity is the only rational or enduring basis of philosophical tolerance; the only condition under which liberality in matters of opinion can be anything better than a polite synonym for indifference between one opinion and another.'

Mill's is itself, as these essays sufficiently evidence, a very distinguished mind. To read them with close attention is an educative experience. This is true as it is not true, for example, of *Biographia Literaria*, that academic classic which is habitually prescribed for study as an initiating and enlightening document. Mill's essays deserve to be called classical for their intrinsic quality; they are models of method and manner. Coleridge was a genius, but his writings cannot be said to be products of a disciplined mind. Mill's pre-eminently are, and they have an intellectual distinction that is at the same time a distinction of character. And the rigorous training that issues in such apparently easy mastery doesn't mean narrowness or dryness. The desiccating rigours and narrownesses of Mill's own education are, of course, notorious; he decribes them himself in the *Autobiography*. But, as the describing shows, he derived from them a kind of profit that had not entered into the intention behind them, so that when he defines Bentham's limitations his phrases represent something more than the 'vague generalities' of vaguely general recognition:

'Nobody's synthesis can be more complete than his analysis. If in his survey of human nature and life he has left any element out, then, wheresoever that element exerts any influence, his conclusions will fail, more or less, in their application.'

'He had a phrase, expressive of the view he took of all moral speculations to which his method had not been applied, or (which he considered the same thing) not founded on a recognition of utility as the moral standard;

this phrase was "vague generalities." Whatever presented itself to him in such a shape he dismissed as unworthy of notice, or dwelt upon only to denounce as absurd. He did not heed, or rather the nature of his mind prevented it from occurring to him, that these generalities contained the whole unanalysed experience of the human race.'

'In many of the most natural and strongest feelings of human nature he had no sympathy; from many of its graver experiences he was altogether cut off; and the faculty by which one mind understands a mind different from itself, and throws itself into the feelings of that other mind, was denied him by his deficiency of Imagination.'

'How much of human nature slumbered in him he knew not, neither can we know. He had never been made alive to the unseen influences which were acting on himself, nor consequently on his fellow-creatures . . . Knowing so little of human feelings, he knew still less of the influences by which those feelings are formed: all the more subtle workings, both of the mind upon itself, and of external things upon the mind, escaped him; and no one, probably, who, in a highly instructed age, ever attempted to give a rule to all human conduct, set out with a more limited conception either of the agencies by which human conduct *is*, or of those by which it *should* be, influenced.'

Mill, then, for all the restrictive rigours of his father's educational experiment shows that he has a sensitive intelligence, informed by introspective subtlety, wide perceptions and a lively historical sense. The pupil of James Mill, and the self-styled Utilitarian, can write the classical appreciation of Coleridge and of the kind

of reaction he stands for against that eighteenth
century which is characterized with such admirable
trenchancy in the Coleridge essay:[1]

'It was natural that a philosophy which anathematized all that had been going on in Europe from
Constantine to Luther, or even to Voltaire, should be
succeeded by another, at once a severe critic of the new
tendencies of society, and an impassioned vindicator of
what was good in the past. This is the easy merit of all
Tory and Royalist writers. But the peculiarity of the
Germano-Coleridgian school, is, that they saw beyond
the immediate controversy, to the fundamental principles
involved in all such controversies . . . They thus produced, not a piece of party advocacy, but a philosophy
of society, in the only form in which it is yet possible,
that of a philosophy of history; not a defence of particular ethical or religious doctrines, but a contribution,
the largest yet made by any class of thinkers, towards
the philosophy of human culture.'

The thinker who could write these complementary
appreciations of the two great opposites might call
himself Utilitarian, and avow that in respect of the
philosophical issue he stands with Locke as against the
transcendentalists, but he was clearly no unqualified
Benthamite. In fact, as we know, he spent his life in
a strenuous endeavour, pursued with magnificent in-
tegrity, to justify his contention that the Benthams
and the Coleridges, 'these two sorts of men, who seem
to be, and believe themselves to be, enemies, are in
reality allies': the side from which he inevitably
worked having been determined by his upbringing,
he worked indefatigably to correct and complete

[1] 'No one can calculate what struggles, which the cause of improvement has yet to undergo, might have been spared if the philosophers
of the eighteenth century had done anything like justice to the Past.'

Utilitarianism by incorporating into it the measure of truth attained by the other side. And here we come to a third main point, for our purpose, about these essays of Mill's: the essayist is not merely a distinguished mind of a different type from Bentham or Coleridge; he is a great representative figure in Victorian intellectual history, and the essays lead on to the *Autobiography*.

Mill's *Autobiography* is a classic that every cultivated person should have read, though very few candidates for Honours in English do, I think, read it. It is certainly a main document for us. The account of the young Mill's early training (and the consequent spiritual crisis) for which it is best known—a *locus classicus* of great significance in any case—has itself a direct bearing on the central themes of the essays and what should be central themes in any study of the Victorian age. The account of his intellectual life that forms the body of the book is an immediately relevant piece of Victorian history that, by reason of the contacts and connexions it records, lends itself peculiarly to the business of educing significant organization in the whole complex field.

Reading, in the account of the Philosophic Radicalism in which Mill made his *début*, of the early *Westminster Review*, we recall that George Eliot became virtual editor of that same review—for there is a continuity, in spite of the vicissitudes of its history—a quarter of a century later. And the connexion is a significant one: George Eliot was never a Benthamite, and the *Westminster Review* she edited was no longer the special organ of Philosophic Radicalism, but her succession in the line leading back to Mill may fairly serve as a reminder that the atmosphere of the intellectual milieu to which she belonged—a milieu very central to the Victorian age—was in a general sense Utilitarian. Mill himself, of course, by that time, was only in a very qualified sense a Utilitarian—or his Utilitarianism was a very different thing from that which he had received from his father. And the hospitality towards new contacts that played so large a part in his development out of pure Benthamism into something pretty much in resonance with George Eliot's unsystematized liberalism shows itself, as recorded in the *Autobiography*, very early.

There was Carlyle, of whose writings he says:

> 'What truths they contained, though of the very kind which I was already receiving from other quarters, were presented in a form and vesture less suited than any other to give them access to a mind trained as mine had been. They seemed a haze of poetry and German metaphysics, in which almost the only clear thing was a strong animosity to most of the opinions which were the basis of my mode of thought; religious scepticism, utilitarianism, the doctrine of circumstances, and the attaching any importance to democracy, logic, or political economy' (p. 148, 'World's Classics' edition, to which the other page references to the *Autobiography* apply also).

But

> 'I did not seek and cultivate Carlyle less on account of the fundamental differences in our philosophy' (p. 149).

We may at first be surprised at his more than tolerance—his respect, and wonder what such a mind could learn from such an opposite. But it *is* respect, and not deference;[1] he exhibits a true and wholly admirable

[1] See *The Impulse to Dominate*, by D. W. Harding; pp. 209 ff.

humility that is at the same time a tenacity in working along his own arduous path:

> 'I did not, however, deem myself a competent judge of Carlyle. I felt that he was a poet, and that I was not; that he was a man of intuition, which I was not; and that as such, he not only saw many things long before me, which I could only, when they were pointed out to me, hobble after and prove, but that it was highly probable he could see many things which were not visible to me even after they were pointed out.'

While this pre-eminently disciplined thinker, a trained logician and analyst, cannot report any particular view or change of view that he owes to Carlyle, he is conscious that that total sense of things—of human experience and the problems implicit in it—upon which analysis operates, and which conditions the analytic process, has responded in some way to Carlyle's imaginative heat and stress.[1] And here the student gets his hint as to the kind of attention Carlyle is worth. It is hard at this date to realize why Carlyle in his own time should have been felt to be so great and profound an influence, and it is bad economy to direct the student in the ordinary way to study him as a key figure of the age. A tenacious inquirer may waste many of his too few hours before deciding that from the great mass of Carlyle's writings no coherent doctrine or system of thought or body of wisdom can be extracted. If Carlyle is to get some attention (and this fairly represents the kind he is worth to the literary student in general), it might reasonably be given by

[1] *Cf.* 'Directly, Carlyle contributed little: but the atmospheric effect of his insistence on personality, immaterial values, and leadership was immense.'—G. M. Young, *Victorian England: Portrait of an Age*, p. 55 (footnote).—This book will be found of great value as a richly suggestive source of themes, and for filling in background. *Carlyle and Mill*, by Emery Neff, is useful for background information.

way of an essay on the debt the young Mill may be imagined to owe him.

Of another early contact the effects were overt and indisputable, that which began in

> '1828 and 1829, when the Coleridgians, in the persons of Maurice and Sterling, made their appearance in the Society as a second Liberal and even Radical party, on totally different grounds from Benthamism and vehemently opposed to it; bringing into these discussions the general doctrines and modes of thought of the European reaction against the philosophy of the eighteenth century' (p. 108).

This refers us back, of course, to the two essays. But it also adds very notably to the system of significant relations. For with Maurice, Christian Socialism and Arnold of Rugby appear on the map, and though (aided by the irresponsible Stracheyan *procédé*) we tend to let the ethos of *Tom Brown's Schooldays* stand for Thomas Arnold, his son has much closer affinities with him than is commonly supposed. So we establish a line running from Coleridge and the German historical critics through Thomas to Matthew Arnold, thus connecting the last—as there is point in doing—with his father's Broad Church liberalism.[1]

If Utilitarianism may be said to have pervaded the intellectual atmosphere in George Eliot's time, so, with equal truth, may Comtism, that most developed expression of the characteristic tendency of the age to replace supernatural religion by the service of humanity. The two are brought together in Mill, who, coming on Comte while extending his acquaintance with the

[1] A line very relevant to George Eliot's development: in fact, for the understanding of her intellectual and religious background, L. Trilling's *Matthew Arnold* provides a valuable supplement to Leslie Stephen's *George Eliot*.

Saint-Simonians (it was before 1830), formed a sustained interest in him, and was a pioneer in getting him known in this country. Mill, of course, never swallowed Positivism whole, and his objections to the system amounted, in essence, to George Eliot's. A great novelist can never be tempted to see a deified Society, as the supremely real thing in relation to which the individual is insignificant,[1] and Mill's individualism was based on grounds of which George Eliot must have approved: Tocqueville (by whom, with so many of his contemporaries, he was profoundly impressed)[2] confirmed his strong sense of the need to safeguard, not only the rights, but the individuality, of the individual against the pressure of a democratic civilization. To preserve and foster variety seemed to him of ultimate importance, and he feared the drive of democratic conditions towards uniformity.[3]

On the other hand, as we go on in the *Autobiography*, we see the original Benthamite individualism modifying itself radically. 'Bentham's idea of the world', he says in the essay on Bentham, 'is that of a collection of persons pursuing each his separate interest or pleasure, and the, prevention of whom from jostling one another more than is unavoidable, may be attempted by hopes and fears derived from three sources—the law, religion, and public opinion.'[4] And

[1] The reader of George Eliot's fiction will have noted many reflective passages the implications of which bear as critically on Comtism as on Utilitarianism. See, for example, *Janet's Repentance*, Chap. XXII.

[2] See the essay on him in *Dissertations and Discussions*, Vol. II.

[3] See *Autobiography*, pp. 214–15.

[4] 'One critic divided the rising generation into fluent Benthamites and muddled Coleridgians. S.T.C. once said to Miss Martineau: "You seem to regard society as an aggregate of individuals." "Of course I do," she replied. There is much history implicit in that encounter, and by 1850 Coleridge had won.' *Victorian England*, p. 68 (footnote).

a much more positive conception of society on his own part is implied in his appreciation of Coleridge. Even at the stage at which he can call himself a Socialist his thinking is still that of a mind for which the individual is the prior fact; he works out from that to the idea of society, and doesn't seem to arrive at any very full inward recognition of the complexities covered by the 'individual-society' antithesis. Yet the development is a sufficiently remarkable one. The individualist, son and pupil of James Mill, refining and deepening his liberalism,[1] comes in the eighteen-forties to avow himself a Socialist:

'In short, I was [had been] a democrat but not the least of a Socialist. We were now much less democrats than I had been, because so long as education continues to be so wretchedly imperfect, we dreaded the ignorance and especially the selfishness and brutality of the mass: but our ideal of ultimate improvement went far beyond Democracy, and would class us decidedly under the general designation of Socialists. While we repudiated with the greatest energy that tyranny of society over the individual which most Socialistic systems are supposed to involve, we yet looked forward to a time when society will no longer be divided into the idle and the industrious; when the rule that they who do not work shall not eat, will be applied not to paupers only, but impartially to all; when the division of the produce of labour, instead of depending, as in so great a degree it now does, on the accident of birth, will be made by concert on an acknowledged principle of justice; and when it will no longer either be, or be thought to be,

[1] 'In this third period (as it may be termed) of my mental progress, which now went hand in hand with hers, my opinions gained equally in breadth and depth, I understood more things, and those which I had understood before, I now understood more thoroughly.' *Auto biography*, p. 194.

impossible for human beings to exert themselves strenu-
ously in procuring benefits which are not to be exclusively their own, but to be shared with the society they
belong to' (p. 196).

It is a development that gives, in its classically
representative way, a most important part of the
intellectual history of the nineteenth century.

By great good luck there lies ready to the student's
hand—or should lie there—a book that, in a way not
less deserving to be described as classically representative, carries on from much the point at which Mill's
Autobiography stops. This is Beatrice Webb's *My
Apprenticeship*. I doubt whether the full distinction
of Mrs. Webb's autobiography is yet generally recognized. The special political and personal associations
that gained it immediate currency as a kind of docu-
mentary classic, the life's record of a notability whose
life has been an important part of recent history, have
tended, I think, to promote something less than a full
recognition. *My Apprenticeship* is one of the classics
of English literature: to say this is perhaps not merely
otiose.

It is much richer in interest than Mill's *Autobiography*. The formative experience of Mrs. Webb's early
life was much richer. Her childhood was not an educational experiment, and she suffered nothing like the
restrictive and starving intellectuality of Mill's upbringing. And as she describes her childhood, its milieu
and its conditions, we recognize in the writer a potential
novelist. In fact, it is not merely because she is a
gifted and highly intellectual woman that, for all the
differences of circumstances, she reminds us of George
Eliot. She too is decidedly a woman, earnest, strong in

18

sympathetic imagination, and religiously given beneath
all the liberal convictions of her intellect. Less easily
intellectual, perhaps, than George Eliot, she canalizes
her earnestness finally in intellectual disciplines, and
achieves her justifying work in a very different field
from that of imaginative art. Yet in her initial drives
and potentialities she is more like George Eliot than the
distinctive achievements of the two women suggest.

Her account of her family and its antecedents is
a representative piece of nineteenth-century social
history:

'The family in which I was born and bred was
curiously typical of the industrial development of the
nineteenth century. My paternal grandfather, Richard
Potter, was the son of a Yorkshire tenant farmer who
increased the profits of farming by keeping a general
provision shop at Tadcaster; my maternal grandfather,
Lawrence Heyworth, belonged to a family of "domes-
tic manufacturers" in Rossendale in Lancashire, the
majority of whom became, in the last decades of the
eighteenth century, "hands" in the new cotton mills.
Evidently my grandfathers were men of initiative and
energy, for they rose rapidly to affluence and industrial
power, one as a Manchester cotton warehouseman, the
other as a Liverpool merchant trading with South
America. Nonconformists in religion, and Radicals in
politics, they both became, after the 1832 Reform Act,
Members of Parliament, intimate friends of Cobden and
Bright, and enthusiastic supporters of the Anti-Corn
Law League. My father graduated in the new London
University, of which my grandfather, as a leading
Unitarian, was one of the founders' (p. 2).[1]

Both grandfathers, we see, had been ardent Cobden-

[1] The page references given here are to the library edition (Long-
mans). The work was once obtainable in the 'Pelican Books'.

ite Radicals. 'But I doubt whether my father was ever a convinced Radical, and some time in the 'sixties he left the Reform Club and joined the Carlton.' Appropriately, he was a financier and company-promoter, prominently occupied in the railway-development of North America. His daughter describes the opulent rootlessness of their lives:

'The same note of perpetual change characterized our social relationships. . . . The world of human intercourse in which I was brought up was in fact an endless series of human beings, unrelated one to another, and only casually connected with the family group—a miscellaneous crowd who came into and went out of our lives, rapidly and unexpectedly. Servants came and went; governesses and tutors came and went; business men of all sorts and degrees, from American railway presidents to Scandinavian timber growers, from British Imperial company-promoters to managers and technicians of local works, came and went; perpetually changing circles of "London Society" acquaintances came and went; intellectuals of all schools of thought, religious, scientific and literary, came and went; my elder sisters' suitors, a series extensive and peculiar, came and went, leaving it is true, in the course of my girlhood, a permanent residue of seven brothers-in-law, who brought with them yet other business, professional and political affiliations, extending and diversifying the perpetually shifting panorama of human nature in society which opened to my view. Our social relations had no roots in the neighbourhood, in vocation, in creed, or for that matter in race; they likened a series of moving pictures —surface impressions without depth—restlessly stimulating in their glittering variety. How expressive of the circumstance of modern profit-making machine enterprise is now its culminating attempt to entertain the world—the ubiquitous cinema!'

Brought up in such a milieu, the 'career' that faced her as the normal one for a good-looking young woman of her class was marriage, and the kind of socially more or less functionless life that is called 'social'. Her account of her struggle, among the pressures and temptations of the environment, to escape such a life ('Dissipation doesn't suit me, morally or physically') and find a vocation is a classical document of certain essential characteristics of human nature that have played an enormous part in history, but not in the 'class' theories of culture of recent fashion. The home itself was not Philistine; in fact, the first part of *My Apprenticeship* serves as a most effective reminder of the actual concrete complexities simplified in Matthew Arnold's threefold classification, which (like Arnold's methods in general) had its point and its efficacy because there was a public capable of appreciating it— one, that is, not exhaustively describable as Philistine or Barbarian.[1] The household of the successful Victorian company-promoter abounded in cultural

---

[1] Just as Mrs. Webb's account, in Chap. III, of her stay with her poor cousins at Bacup, the small mill-town, forces us to recognize how much more there was in Nonconformist religion than Arnold's 'the Dissidence of Dissent' takes cognizance of. It is a valuable document. The whole account of the community deserves close attention. She notes the part of Dissent in the Co-operative Movement and in the history of English democracy generally:

'There is an immense amount of co-operation in the whole of this district; the stores seem to succeed well, both as regards supplying the people with cheap articles and as savings banks paying good interest. Of course, I am just in the centre of the dissenting organization; and as our host is the chapel keeper and entertains all the ministers who come here, I hear all about the internal management. Each chapel, even of the same denomination, manages its own affairs; and there are monthly meetings of all the members (male and female) to discuss questions of expenditure, etc. In fact each chapel is a self-governing community, regulating not only chapel matters but overlooking the private life of its members. One cannot help feeling what an excellent thing these

interests and intellectual stimulus—to distracting excess, even, it might be suggested. This is a characteristic note:

> 'And whether we girls took down from the well-filled library shelves the *Confessions of St. Augustine* or those of Jean Jacques Rousseau, whether the parcel from Hatchett's contained the latest novels by Guy de Maupassant and Emile Zola or the learned tomes of Auguste Comte or Ernest Renan; whether we ordered from the London Library or from Mudie's a pile of books on Eastern religions, or a heterogeneous selection of what I will call "yellow" literature, was determined by our own choice or by the suggestion of any casual friend or acquaintance. When we complained to my father that a book we wanted to read was banned by the libraries: "Buy it, my dear," was his automatic answer.'

Such a milieu, whatever its shortcomings, was not Philistine. And, for all the suggested heterogeneity of the interests and influences, there were predominant positive characters manifested in the sum of them: the company-promoter's home, in fact, gives us representative glimpses, not of Victorian Philistinism, but of Victorian intellectual culture in the period of George Eliot's established glory:

> dissenting organizations have been for educating this class for self-government' (p. 161).

> 'Still, living actually with these people has given me an insight that is difficult to express in words, into higher working-class life —with all its charm of direct thinking, honest work and warm feeling; and above all, taught me the real part played by religion in making the English people, and of dissent teaching them the art of self-government, or rather serving as a means to develop their capacity for it. It saddens one to think that the religious faith that has united them together with a strong bond of spiritual effort and sustained them individually, throwing its warmth of light into the more lonely and unloved lives, is destined to pass away' (p. 170).

22

'In the particular social and intellectual environment in which I lived, this stream of tendencies culminated in Auguste Comte's union of the "religion of humanity" with a glorification of science, in opposition to both theology and metaphysics, as the final stage in the development of the human intellect. And once again I note that the reading of books was in my case directed and supplemented by friendly intercourse with the men and women most concerned with the subject-matter of the books. As a student I was familiar with the writings of the most famous of the English disciples and admirers of Auguste Comte. I had learnt my lesson from George Henry Lewes. I delighted in John Stuart Mill's *Autobiography*, and had given to his *System of Logic* and *Principles of Political Economy* an assiduous though somewhat strained attention. Above all, the novels of George Eliot had been eagerly read and discussed in the family circle. But I doubt whether my sister Margaret and I would have ordered from the London Library all the works of Comte himself if it had not been for a continuously friendly intercourse with the Frederic Harrisons. . . .'

The great friend of the family and frequenter of the house—'philosopher on the hearth'—was Herbert Spencer, and it was he above all others who encouraged the young aspirant and initiated her into the disciplined life of the mind. As for the nature of his influence:

'He taught me to look on all social institutions exactly as if they were plants or animals—things that could be observed, classified and explained, and the action of which could to some extent be foretold if one knew enough about them.'

The pupil who 'reminded him of George Eliot' (p. 29) provided her own corrective to an influence of this

23

kind, for if she resembled the great novelist it was not merely in the intellectual grasp and stamina that so impressed Spencer; she was profoundly and imaginatively interested in the individual life,[1] and, as she herself notes (and as much in her book confirms), she might herself have been a novelist:

> 'From my diary entries I infer that, if I had followed my taste and my temperament (I will not say my talent), I should have become, not a worker in the field of sociology, but a descriptive psychologist; either in the novel, to which I was from time to time tempted; or (if I had been born thirty years later) in a scientific analysis of the mental make-up of individual men and women, and their behaviour under particular conditions.'[2]

The passage (p. 119) in which she elaborates the point that 'Something beyond keen intellectual faculty is necessary to the psychologist and sociologist' might have been written by George Eliot:

> 'Therefore I solemnly dedicate my energies for the next five months to the cultivation of the social instincts —trusting that the good dæmon within me will keep me from all vulgarity of mind, insincerity and falseness. I

[1] '. . . although I realized the value of physical science as a training in scientific method, the whole subject-matter of natural science bored me. I was not interested in rocks and plants, grubs and animals, not even in man considered merely as a biped, with the organs of a biped. What roused and absorbed my curiosity were men and women, regarded—if I may use an old-fashioned word—as "souls," their past and present conditions of life, their thoughts and feelings and their constantly changing behaviour.'

[2] She goes on: 'For there begin to appear in my diary, from 1882 onwards, realistic scenes from country and town life, descriptions of manners and morals, analytic portraits of relations and friends— written, not with any view to self-education, as were my abstracts, extracts and reviews, but merely because I enjoyed writing them. It is, however, significant that these sketches from life nearly always concern the relation of the individual to some particular social organization; to big enterprise, or to Parliament, to the profession of law, or of medicine, or of the Church.'

would like to go amongst men and women with a determination to know them; to humbly observe and consider
their characteristics; always remembering how much
there is in the most inferior individual which is outside
and beyond one's understanding. Every fresh intimacy
strengthens the conviction of one's own powerlessness
to comprehend fully any other nature, even when one
watches it with love. And without sympathy there is an
impassable barrier to the real knowledge of the inner
workings which guide the outer actions of human beings.
Sympathy, or rather *accepted* sympathy, is the only
instrument for the dissection of character. All great
knowers and describers of human nature must have possessed this instrument. The perfection of the instrument
depends no doubt on a purely intellectual quality, analytical imagination—this, again, originating in subjective
complexity of motive and thought. But unless this latter
quality is possessed to an extraordinary degree, insight
into other natures is impossible, unless we subordinate
our interest in self and its workings to a greater desire
to understand others. Therefore the resolution which
has been growing in my mind is, that I will fight against
my natural love of impressing others, and prepare my
mind to receive impressions. And as fast as I receive
impressions I will formulate them, thereby avoiding
the general haziness of outline which follows a period
of receptivity without an attempt of expression' (MS.
diary, February 22, 1883).

The relation between this and such notes as the
following, in which (with references to the inadequacies
of such 'disciplined explorations of the varieties of
human experience' as claimed academic recognition—
psychology, and so on) she describes her attempts to
train herself in observation and analysis, is obvious,
as is the bearing of all these parts of *My Apprenticeship*
on the importance of literary studies as, not self-

sufficient, but central to a properly conceived liberal education:

> 'For any detailed description of the complexity of human nature, of the variety and mixture in human motive, of the insurgence of instinct in the garb of reason, of the multifarious play of the social environment on the individual ego and of the individual ego on the social environment, I had to turn to novelists and poets. . . .'

That a literary training, involving its proper discipline of intelligence (for there is one), would be very relevant to the essential qualifications of psychologists and sociologists—this is a contention the grounds for which are pretty plainly hinted at in such texts as these from *My Apprenticeship*. Correlatively, they hint at the ways in which, in a University English School as it should be, literary studies would lead outside themselves into other fields and other disciplines.

Beatrice Potter's kind of interest in the individual life, her novelist's interest in the concrete, also helped to save her from any bondage to her mentor's individualism. For Spencer, so far from countenancing Mill's kind of development towards Socialism, made, in *Man versus the State*, his protest against all compromise. That the author of *First Principles* should, in spite of his generalizing preoccupations with Biology, Psychology and Sociology, have been able to persist in an extreme individualism is a tribute to the strength of the Utilitarian tradition. No doubt the promptings of his essential influence, followed up, were themselves calculated to lead his pupil to take less atomistic views of the relations between the individual and society. But the gifts that made her so unlike her teacher, and more like George Eliot than he most likely appreciated, must have speeded her escape from *laissez-faire*. The intelligence that recognized so clearly the rôles of sympathy and imaginative insight, and that turned for the best instruction in 'the complexity of human nature' and 'the multifarious play of the social environment on the individual ego, and of the individual ego on the social environment' to the poets and the novelists couldn't have rested in Utilitarian individualism, or, contemplating slump-induced misery, have shared the simple faith of *The Times*: 'There is no one to blame for this; it is the result of Nature's simplest laws!'

But the student in making this point will perhaps be aware of a certain irony as he thinks of the characteristic modern development with which her life's-work—that devoted life's-work (so different from a novelist's) in which she found her vocation—is associated. Certainly it is in a peculiarly suggestive way that her account of her apprenticeship brings together for his contemplation the unchastened individualism of the world into which she was born and that endless growth in the range and complexity of state organization and bureaucratic control which makes the individual feel so helpless and so insignificant in the modern world. And, though they were old when they permitted themselves the enthusiasm, or virtual complicity, of that docile 'report', one notes as possibly a radical implicit criticism of the ethos of 'the Webbs' that the life's-work for which Spencer inaugurated the training ended in *Soviet Communism: A New Civilization*. ('Its organizational structure is surely the most complicated known to political science'—[the Preface].)

Spencer was not the only presence in the home, or the most intimate, of *laissez-faire* individualism—the pure, conscious and uncompromising creed. Here is Mrs. Webb's account of her mother:

'An ardent student of Adam Smith, Malthus, and particularly of Nassau Senior, she had been brought up in the strictest sect of Utilitarian economists. In middle life she had translated some of the essays of her friend Michel Chevalier, who represented the French variant of orthodox political economy, a variant which caricatured the dogmatic faith in a beneficent self-interest. And my mother practised what she preached. Tested by economy in money and time she was an admirable expenditor of the family income: she never visited the servants' quarters and seldom spoke to any servant other than her own maid. She acted by deputy, training each daughter to carry out a carefully thought-out plan of the most economical supply of the best-regulated demand. Her intellect told her that to pay more than the market rate, to exact fewer than the customary hours or insist on less than the usual strain—even if it could be proved that these conditions were injurious to the health and happiness of the persons concerned—was an act of self-indulgence, a defiance of nature's laws which would bring disaster on the individual and the community. Similarly, it was the bounden duty of every citizen to better his social status; to ignore those beneath him, and to aim steadily at the top rung of the social ladder. Only by this persistent pursuit by each individual of his own and his family's interest would the highest general level of civilization be attained. It was on this issue that she and Herbert Spencer found themselves in happy accord. No one of the present generation realizes with what sincerity and fervour these doctrines were held by the representative men and women of the mid-Victorian middle class. "The man who sells his cow too cheap goes to hell" still epitomizes, according to John Butler Yeats, "the greater part of the religion of

28

Belfast"—that last backwater of the sanctimonious commercialism of the nineteenth century.'[1]

Against this background the force of mind and character represented by Mill's development becomes more fully appreciable.

Of course, Mrs. Potter's rigid orthodoxy and Mill's intellectually strenuous modification do not exhaustively represent the Utilitarianism of the Victorian age, if we are to talk of Utilitarianism as having been pervasive. And this is the point at which to suggest that the postulated study-group ought to sketch for itself in brief the history of Utilitarian thought and its influence. Perhaps, as a measure of economy, a tough and efficient reader or two might be detailed to extract from Halévy's *Growth of Philosophic Radicalism* for the benefit of the group the main points about the origins of Benthamism. For Bentham, of course, brought together a great deal of representative thinking, and an account of his affiliations and connexions is a large part of the intellectual history of the eighteenth century. The history as given by Halévy is loaded with names, English and French, but our deputed inquirers could without great difficulty elicit the main lines and elements. In particular they would note the coming together of what is represented by the name of Adam Smith with what may be represented by the name of Newton. Not that Newton himself contributed directly to Benthamism in the way in which Adam Smith did; I am thinking of the ambition to do for human nature and human affairs what the immortal Newton, the acclaimed genius of the new physical science, had done for astronomy.

This ambition, we know, forms a characteristic

[1] *My Apprenticeship*, p, 14.

accompaniment of the Benthamite ethos. Literary students—ours are literary in the first place—will have come on it in the work of Dr. I. A. Richards; work that ought to be seen—even by literary students —in its relation to the tradition it belongs to. Approached in the way suggested, the offered psychological criticism of *The Principles of Literary Criticism*, in fact, is likely to strike them as curiously contemporary with Bentham. In the later phase, that represented by *Coleridge on Imagination*, the ambition takes a subtler form. The cue for the book itself, our students will note, was given by Mill's pronouncement about Bentham and Coleridge in the essay on the latter: 'Whoever could master the premises and combine the methods of both, would possess the entire English philosophy of their age.' They will note too that Dr. Richards's way of combining is to 'restate Coleridge in terms of Bentham', and perhaps they will go on to judge that this is a very different process from that to which Mill devoted his life;[1] a very different kind of thing from Mill's endeavour to modify crude Benthamite Utilitarianism into something fully consonant with an appreciation of Coleridge. They are likely, I think, to judge with some emphasis that the effect of 'restatement' is to *replace* Coleridge by Bentham.

I am here, of course, expressing my own view[2] (which at some time, in such radical matters, one is bound to do). And I will add further that the approach

[1] What more is needed concerning Mill's development will be found very accessible in Leslie Stephen's *The English Utilitarians*, Vol. III: 'John Stuart Mill ''.

[2] It will be found expressed at length in an examination of *Coleridge on Imagination* that appeared in *Scrutiny* for March, 1935 (Vol. III, No. 4).

I have been indicating conduces, I think, to a due precipitation of the suspicion that the subtleties of semasiology clothe an essentially Benthamite spirit— Benthamite in a field in which to be Benthamite is to be indifferent to essential elements (essential, at any rate, from the Coleridgean point of view) in the problems one offers to be tackling. Certainly (it seems to me) Basic English exemplifies the practical spirit of Benthamism—'It can teach the means of organizing and regulating the merely *business* part of the social arrangements'[1]—applying itself to matters where its indifference to essential human interests that are involved is calculated to have, for those interests, disastrous consequences.

Whether these judgments are wholly endorsed or not, it is an important line of intellectual history that comes up with them. Adam Smith's name brings up the relation of Utilitarianism to social, economic and political history. The historical significance of the *laissez-faire* individualism that counts for so much in the Utilitarian tradition is plain enough: a society in which the classes associated with the expanding

[1] P. 73 below. *Cf*. 'If Bentham's theory of life can do so little for the individual, what can it do for society?

'It will enable a society which has attained a certain state of spiritual development, and the maintenance of which in that state is otherwise provided for, to prescribe the rules by which it may protect its material interests. It will do nothing (except sometimes as an instrument in the hands of a higher doctrine) for the spiritual interests of society; nor does it suffice of itself even for the material interests. That which alone causes any material interests to exist, which alone enables any body of human beings to exist as a society, is national character . . . All he can do is but to indicate means by which in any given state of the national mind, the material interests of society can be protected; saving the question, of which others may judge, whether the use of those means would have, on the national character, any injurious influence' (p. 72).

The whole passage deserves pondering in relation to Matthew Arnold's preoccupations.

capitalist enterprise of eighteenth-century England represented the stir of new energy and naturally tended to see government, identified as it was with the persisting paternal and mercantilist habits of the vestigial old order, social and economic, as mainly an obstructive and interfering nuisance, and to favour a minimal conception of it. Mill in his *Coleridge* says (pp. 136 ff. below):

'The State, again, was no longer considered, according to the old ideal, as a concentration of the force of all the individuals of the nation in the hands of certain of its members, in order to the accomplishment of whatever could be best accomplished by systematic co-operation. It was found that the State was a bad judge of the wants of society; that it in reality cared very little for them; and when it attempted anything beyond that police against crime, and arbitration of disputes, which are indispensable to social existence, the private sinister interest of some class or individual was usually the prompter of its proceedings . . . Government altogether was regarded as a necessary evil, and was required to hide itself, to make itself as little felt as possible. The cry of the people was not "help us," "guide us," "do for us the things we cannot do, and instruct us, that we may do well those which we can"—and truly such requirements from such rulers would have been a bitter jest: the cry was "let us alone." Power to decide questions of *meum* and *tuum*, to protect society from open violence, and from some of the most dangerous modes of fraud, could not be withheld; these functions the Government was left in possession of, and to these it became the expectation of the public that it should confine itself.'

But the significance in relation to social and economic history of Bentham's thought is a great deal wider than can be suggested by referring to Adam Smith and *laissez-faire*. Mill, in the essay on him, gives it in a general way here (p. 41), in discussing him as the 'great questioner of things established':

'Who, before Bentham (whatever controversies might exist on points of detail) dared to speak disrespectfully, in express terms, of the British Constitution, or the English Law? He did so; and his arguments and his example together encouraged others. We do not mean that his writings caused the Reform Bill or that the Appropriation Clause owns him as its parent: the changes which have been made, and the greater changes which will be made, in our institutions, are not the work of philosophers, but of the interests and instincts of large portions of society recently grown into strength. But Bentham gave voice to those interests and instincts: until he spoke out, those who found our institutions unsuited to them did not dare to say so, did not dare consciously to think so; they had never heard the excellence of those institutions questioned by cultivated men, by men of acknowledged intellect; and it is not in the nature of uninstructed minds to resist the united authority of the instructed. Bentham broke the spell.'

For all that, Bentham was politically no Radical, but rather Tory-inclined for a great part of his life. It was James Mill who, in the early years of the nineteenth century, made Benthamism a political force, and identified Bentham with Philosophic Radicalism. The history of the central part played by Philosophic Radicalism in the movement of agitation, political education and organized pressure that led up to the Reform Act of 1832 is to be found in Halévy's book. There is no need here to suggest what other reading should be done in this connexion; suitable tips would be readily gathered in consultation with qualified authority.[1] It is, however, in place to say that the members of our study-group, following their special focal interests through this critical period of English history, would be well disposed and sensitized for improving their general grasp of it.

The Reform Act once achieved, the common aim that had held together the heterogeneous forces combined to achieve it was gone. The class that had risen to assured political power had naturally no enthusiasm for further reforms—reforms, that is, tending towards the sharing of its privileges and the reduction of its power. Apart from Municipal Reform, in which, of course, they were very much concerned, the one great distinctive achievement of the Philosophic Radicals consequent upon the act was, significantly, the new Poor Law, symbolic embodiment of all that was most rationally and righteously inhuman in orthodox Utilitarianism, with its implacable Malthusian logic. Utilitarianism, in fact, provided the sanction for the complacent selfishness and comfortable obtuseness of the prosperous classes in the great age of Progress: they were protected by righteous rationality from the importunities of imaginative sympathy. We have had an illustration of the creed held simply and sincerely, and so in a sense respectably, in Mrs. Webb's account of her mother. The supreme document in creative literature, where Victorian Utilitarianism and its part in Victorian civilization are in question, is *Hard Times*, with the grim play of its title. This masterpiece, as I have

---

[1] *William Cobbett*, by G. D. H. Cole, and *The Life of Francis Place*, by Graham Wallas, oughtn't in any case to be missed. Cobbett, it may be said here, should be a more substantial value for the 'English' student than he commonly is, and any specially designed 'English' library should contain his works.

argued elsewhere (in *The Great Tradition*), offers itself as a key work for the critical study of fiction. Taking stock of its superiority in the Dickensian *œuvre* as a work of art, the critic finds himself considering those aspects of the Victorian world which exercised so strong a compulsion upon Dickens's creative powers, and controlled them, for once, to a profound and sustained seriousness of response. The close relations between literary criticism and extra-literary studies invited in the appreciation of *Hard Times* need, then, no insisting on; the general nature of the opportunity is plain.

Here I will only note that Gradgrind and Bounderby give us, in significant association, two aspects of Victorian Utilitarianism. In Gradgrind, as in Beatrice Webb's mother, it is a matter of principle; a serious creed, if a repellent one. But Gradgrind consorts freely and uncritically with Josiah Bounderby—marries his daughter to him, in fact. And Bounderby is 'rugged individualism' in its most gross and brutal form. Yet Gradgrind is represented as a kind of James Mill, a stern and practical theorist, who gives his children, from intellectual conviction, an education like that suffered by Mill's son, and recorded in the *Autobiography*. And the justice of this vision of the tendency of James Mill's kind of Utilitarianism, as manifested in later history, can hardly be questioned.

But the Utilitarianism of the Victorian age was something more than a matter of Bounderby, Gradgrind and John Stuart Mill. What may fairly be called a Utilitarian ethos was pervasive, and can be found in representative figures who would not have called themselves Utilitarians. Is it not there, for instance, in Macaulay, the critic of James Mill? The student might ponder this question, while looking through the third chapter of the *History*[1] (considering, perhaps, along with it Chapter VI of Firth's *Commentary on Macaulay's History of England*).

This, then, is the kind of field that co-ordinates itself round John Stuart Mill, approached in the way suggested. For the other main figure—that to be set over against Mill—I have already proposed Matthew Arnold as the obvious choice. Set study of Carlyle or Ruskin, for instance, would be bad economy. What Carlyle[2] stands for or against (it is apt to seem mainly that) can be summarized fairly briefly, voluminous as he is. Ruskin's destructive analysis of the orthodox political economy was a great and noble achievement, entitling him to enduring honour, but it can be worth few students' while to follow it through at any length in the original documents: it is fairly easy to say what his place and significance are.[3] Arnold, on the other hand, cannot be summarized. I say this with an eye, not on his weaknesses and inconsistencies as a thinker, but on his essential strength. And here we have a reason for his being worth special study. He is not easy to do justice to, and to attempt it seriously is to refine one's understanding of the nature of intelligence. For, though he is in so many ways so unlike Mill, he

[1] The essay by Matthew Arnold on Falkland in *Mixed Essays* might well be read in conjunction with this. (Arnold, of course, has in various places some very useful characterizing references to Macaulay.) Here too would be a good place to introduce H. Butterfield's *The Whig Interpretation of History* (along with which should be read 'The Interpretation of History' by A. J. Woolford in *Scrutiny*, Vol. XIII, No. 1).

[2] Leslie Stephen's essay on him in *Hours in a Library*, Vol. III, is very good, and J. M. Robertson's in *Modern Humanists Reconsidered* is worth looking up, as is his essay on Ruskin.

[3] J. A. Hobson's *John Ruskin* is to be recommended. B. E. Lippincott's *Victorian Critics of Democracy* (Oxford University Press), dealing with Carlyle, Ruskin, Arnold and others, will be found very useful.

too stands for intelligence (as the contrast with Carlyle brings out). Unlike Mill, he is not a systematic thinker, he represents no strict intellectual discipline, he doesn't go in for sharpness and completeness of analysis or full and clear statement of principle, and he is not preoccupied with consistency. This might seem to leave little that can be claimed for him—a conclusion, by all appearances, that has been pretty widely entertained, though he has contrived to command attention and remain a live author as Carlyle, I think, has not, and Ruskin has not (in spite of the qualities of *Præterita* that should have made it a current classic and that make it a document to be read with the *Autobiography* of Mill and *My Apprenticeship*).

The difficulty of being fair to him, a difficulty that every one interested in him must have experienced, is illustrated at the most distinguished level by Mr. T. S. Eliot in *The Use of Poetry and the Use of Criticism.* It is illustrated in a much less respectable way by Raleigh, whose essay in *Some Authors* should be known to the student as a *locus classicus* for the unscrupulous and silly malice, revealing a radical dislike of live intelligence, that so often goes with a reputation for 'brilliance' in the academic mind.[1] It is illustrated with honest and forthright crudity in another essay the student might well look at: that by J. M. Robertson in *Modern Humanists Reconsidered.* The obtuseness manifested in the march of Robertson's relentless logic has a clear relation to his demand for an equivalent logic in Arnold. And here we have the clue to the general

[1] It is significant that Robert Bridges, whose performance as friend and editor of Gerard Manley Hopkins so notably exemplifies the 'academic mind', should refer to Arnold as 'Mr. Kidglove-Cocksure', for which show of animus he is rebuked by Hopkins (*The Letters of Gerard Manley Hopkins to Robert Bridges*, XCVII).

unfairness from which Arnold has suffered: he has been judged by inappropriate criteria, as if he offered what he doesn't, and as if a critic who fails of logical rigour and strictness of definition is left with no respectable function of intelligence that he might be performing.

The flexibility, the sensitiveness, the constant delicacy of touch for the concrete in all its complexity, the intelligence that is inseparably one with an alert and fine sense of value—these qualities, however severe the criticism to be brought against him, are exemplified by Arnold; and it is the reader of literary critical training who should find them a challenge to appreciation. Such a student will recall that in the essay, *The Function of Criticism*, it is more than the function of literary criticism that is being discussed; it is the general function of critical intelligence in a civilized community: Arnold is defining a function that extends the habit, the methods and the qualifications of a good literary critic to the more general field. Our postulated student, who is to bring with him the training of a literary critic, may profitably inquire how far Arnold's writings exemplify such an extension.

And this brings me to a final emphasis on the intention of these notes: the student, I repeat, is in the first place a student of literature. I am assuming that at the centre of the work here in view there will be a critical study of the novels of George Eliot, and I have been trying to suggest the kind of work—the approach, the development and the organization— that should, I think, replace that represented (to take an instance in front of me) by the prescription for 'special study' of the English novel over two or three Victorian decades—a usual kind of prescription that seems to me radically and wastefully misconceived.

BENTHAM

THERE are two men, recently deceased, to whom their country is indebted not only for the greater part of the important ideas which have been thrown into circulation among its thinking men in their time, but for a revolution in its general modes of thought and investigation. These men, dissimilar in almost all else, agreed in being closet-students—secluded in a peculiar degree, by circumstances and character, from the business and intercourse of the world: and both were, through a large portion of their lives, regarded by those who took the lead in opinion (when they happened to hear of them) with feelings akin to contempt. But they were destined to renew a lesson given to mankind by every age, and always disregarded—to show that speculative philosophy, which to the superficial appears a thing so remote from the business of life and the outward interests of men, is in reality the thing on earth which most influences them, and in the long run overbears every other influence save those which it must itself obey. The writers of whom we speak have never been read by the multitude; except for the more slight of their works, their readers have been few: but they have been the teachers of the teachers; there is hardly to be found in England an individual of any importance in the world of mind, who (whatever opinions he may have afterwards adopted) did not first learn to think from one of these two; and though their influences have but begun to diffuse themselves through these intermediate channels over society at large, there is already scarcely a publication of any consequence addressed to the educated classes, which, if these persons had not existed, would not have been different from what it is. These men are, Jeremy Bentham and Samuel Taylor Coleridge—the two great seminal minds of England in their age.

No comparison is intended here between the minds or influences of these remarkable men: this were impossible unless there were first formed a complete judgment of each, considered apart. It is our intention to attempt, on the present occasion, an estimate of one of them; the only one, a complete edition of whose works is yet in progress, and who, in the classification which may be made of all writers into Progressive and Conservative, belongs to the same division with ourselves. For although they were far too great men to be correctly designated by either appellation exclusively, yet in the main, Bentham was a Progressive philosopher, Coleridge a Conservative one. The influence of the former has made itself felt chiefly on minds of the Progressive class; of the latter, on those of the Conservative: and the two systems of concentric circles which the shock given by them is spreading over the ocean of mind, have only just begun to meet and intersect. The writings of both contain severe lessons to their own side, on many of the errors and faults they are addicted to: but to Bentham it was given to discern more particularly those truths with which existing doctrines and institutions were at variance; to Coleridge, the neglected truths which lay *in* them.

A man of great knowledge of the world, and of the highest reputation for practical talent and sagacity among the official men of his time (himself no follower of Bentham, nor of any partial or exclusive school whatever) once said to us, as the result of his observation, that to Bentham more than to any other source might be traced the questioning spirit, the disposition to demand the *why* of everything, which had gained so much ground and was producing such important consequences in these times. The more this assertion is examined, the more true it will be found. Bentham has been in this age and country the great questioner of things established. It is by the influence of the modes of thought with which his writings inoculated a considerable number of thinking men, that the yoke of authority has been broken, and innumerable opinions, formerly received on tradition as incontestable, are put upon their defence, and required to give an account of themselves. Who, before Bentham, (whatever controversies might exist on points of detail,) dared to speak disrespectfully, in express terms, of the British Constitution, or the English Law? He did so; and his arguments and his example together encouraged others. We do not mean that his writings caused the Reform Bill, or that the Appropriation Clause owns him as its parent: the changes which have been made, and the greater changes which will be made, in our institutions, are not the work of philosophers, but of the interests and instincts of large portions of society recently grown into strength. But Bentham gave voice to those interests and instincts: until he spoke out, those who found our institutions unsuited to them did not dare to say so, did not dare consciously to think so; they had never heard the excellence of those institutions questioned by cultivated men, by men of acknowledged intellect; and it is not in the nature of uninstructed minds to resist the united authority of the instructed. Bentham broke the spell. It was not Bentham by his own writings; it was Bentham through the minds and pens which those writings fed—through the men in more direct contact with the world, into whom his spirit passed. If the superstition about ancestorial wisdom has fallen into decay; if the public are grown familiar with the idea that their laws and institutions are in great part not the product of intellect and virtue, but of modern corruption grafted upon ancient barbarism; if the hardiest innovation is no longer scouted *because* it is an innovation—establishments no longer considered sacred because they are establishments—it will be found that those who have accustomed the public mind to these ideas have learnt them in Bentham's school, and that the assault on ancient institutions has been, and is, carried on for the most part with his weapons. It matters not although these thinkers, or indeed thinkers of any description, have been but scantily found among the persons prominently and ostensibly at the head of the Reform movement. All movements, except directly revolutionary ones, are headed, not by those who originate them, but by those who know best how to compromise between the old opinions and the new. The father of English innovation, both in doctrines and in institutions, is Bentham: he is the great *subversive*, or, in the language of continental philosophers, the great *critical*, thinker of his age and country.

We consider this, however, to be not his highest title to fame. Were this all, he were only to be ranked among the lowest order of the potentates of mind—the negative, or destructive philosophers; those who can perceive what is false, but not what is true; who awaken the human mind to the inconsistencies and absurdities of time-sanctioned opinions and institutions, but substitute nothing in the place of what they take away. We have no desire to undervalue the services of such persons: mankind have been deeply indebted to them; nor will there ever be a lack of work for them, in a world in which so many false things are believed, in which so many which have been true, are believed long after they have ceased to be true. The qualities, however, which fit men for perceiving anomalies, without perceiving the truths which would rectify them, are not among the rarest of endowments. Courage, verbal acuteness, command over the forms of argumentation, and a popular style, will make, out of the shallowest man, with a sufficient lack of reverence, a considerable negative philosopher. Such men have never been wanting in periods of culture; and the period in which Bentham formed his early impressions was emphatically their reign, in proportion to its barrenness in the more noble products of the human mind. An age of formalism in the Church and corruption in the State, when the most valuable part of the meaning of traditional doctrines had faded from the minds even of those who retained from habit a mechanical belief in them, was the time to raise up all kinds of sceptical philosophy. Accordingly, France had Voltaire, and his school of negative thinkers, and England (or rather Scotland) had the profoundest negative thinker on record, David Hume: a man, the peculiarities of whose mind qualified him to detect failure of proof, and want of logical consistency, at a depth which French sceptics, with their comparatively feeble powers of analysis and abstraction, stopt far short of, and which German subtlety could alone thoroughly appreciate, or hope to rival.

If Bentham had merely continued the work of Hume, he would scarcely have been heard of in philosophy; for he was far inferior to Hume in Hume's qualities, and was in no respect fitted to excel as a metaphysician. We must not look for subtlety, or the power of recondite analysis, among his intellectual characteristics. In the former quality, few great thinkers have ever been so deficient; and to find the latter, in any considerable measure, in a mind acknowledging any kindred with his, we must have recourse to the late Mr. Mill—a man who united the great qualities of the metaphysicians of the eighteenth century, with others of a different complexion, admirably qualifying him to complete and correct their work. Bentham had not these peculiar gifts; but he possessed others, not inferior, which were not possessed by any of his precursors; which have made him a source of light to a generation which has far outgrown their influence, and, as we called him, the chief subversive thinker of an age which has long lost all that they could subvert.

To speak of him first as a merely negative philosopher—as one who refutes illogical arguments, exposes sophistry, detects contradiction and absurdity; even in that capacity there was a wide field left vacant for him by Hume, and which he has occupied to an unprecedented extent; the field of practical abuses. This was Bentham's peculiar province: to this he was called by the whole bent of his disposition: to carry the warfare against absurdity into things practical. His · was an essentially practical mind. It was by practical abuses that his mind was first turned to speculation—by the abuses of the profession which was chosen for him, that of the law. He has himself stated what particular abuse first gave that shock to his mind, the recoil of which has made the whole mountain of abuse totter; it was the custom of making the client pay for three attendances in the office of a Master in Chancery, when only one was given. The law, he found, on examination, was full of such things. But were these discoveries of his? No; they were known to every lawyer who practised, to every judge who sat on the bench, and neither before nor for long after did they cause any apparent uneasiness to the consciences of these learned persons, nor hinder them from asserting, whenever occasion offered, in books, in parliament, or on the bench, that the law was the perfection of reason. During so many generations, in each of which thousands of well-educated young men were successively placed in Bentham's position and with Bentham's opportunities, he alone was found with sufficient moral sensibility and self-reliance to say to himself that these things, however profitable they might be, were frauds, and that between them and himself there should be a gulf fixed. To this rare union of self-reliance and moral sensibility we are indebted for all that Bentham has done. Sent to Oxford by his father at the unusually early age of fifteen—required, on admission, to declare his belief in the Thirty-nine Articles—he felt it necessary to examine them; and the examination suggested scruples, which he sought to get removed, but instead of the satisfaction he expected, was told that it was not for boys like him to set up their judgment against the great men of the Church. After a struggle, he signed; but the impression that he had done an immoral act, never left him; he considered himself to have committed a falsehood, and throughout life he never relaxed in his indignant

45

denunciations of all laws which command such falsehoods, all institutions which attach rewards to them.

By thus carrying the war of criticism and refutation, the conflict with falsehood and absurdity, into the field of practical evils, Bentham, even if he had done nothing else, would have earned an important place in the history of intellect. He carried on the warfare without intermission. To this, not only many of his most piquant chapters, but some of the most finished of his entire works, are entirely devoted: the 'Defence of Usury'; the 'Book of Fallacies'; and the onslaught upon Blackstone, published anonymously under the title of 'A Fragment on Government', which, though a first production, and of a writer afterwards so much ridiculed for his style, excited the highest admiration no less for its composition than for its thoughts, and was attributed by turns to Lord Mansfield, to Lord Camden, and (by Dr. Johnson) to Dunning, one of the greatest masters of style among the lawyers of his day. These writings are altogether original; though of the negative school, they resemble nothing previously produced by negative philosophers; and would have sufficed to create for Bentham, among the subversive thinkers of modern Europe, a place peculiarly his own. But it is not these writings that constitute the real distinction between him and them. There was a deeper difference. It was that they were purely negative thinkers, he was positive: they only assailed error, he made it a point of conscience not to do so until he thought he could plant instead the corresponding truth. Their character was exclusively analytic, his was synthetic. They took for their starting-point the received opinion on any subject, dug round it with their logical implements, pronounced its foundations defective, and condemned it: he began *de novo*, laid his own foundations deeply and firmly, built up his own structure, and bade mankind compare the two; it was when he had solved the problem himself, or thought he had done so, that he declared all other solutions to be erroneous. Hence, what they produced will not last; it must perish, much of it has already perished, with the errors which it exploded: what he did has its own value, by which it must outlast all errors to which it is opposed. Though we may reject, as we often must, his practical conclusions, yet his premises, the collections of facts and observations from which his conclusions were drawn, remain for ever, a part of the materials of philosophy.

A place, therefore, must be assigned to Bentham among the masters of wisdom, the great teachers and permanent intellectual ornaments of the human race. He is among those who have enriched mankind with imperishable gifts; and although these do not transcend all other gifts, nor entitle him to those honours 'above all Greek, above all Roman fame', which by a natural reaction against the neglect and contempt of the world, many of his admirers were once disposed to accumulate upon him, yet to refuse an admiring recognition of what he was, on account of what he was not, is a much worse error, and one which, pardonable in the vulgar, is no longer permitted to any cultivated and instructed mind.

If we were asked to say, in the fewest possible words, what we conceive to be Bentham's place among these great intellectual benefactors of humanity; what he was, and what he was not; what kind of service he did and did not render to truth; we should say—he was

not a great philosopher, but he was a great reformer
in philosophy. He brought into philosophy something
which it greatly needed, and for want of which it was
at a stand. It was not his doctrines which did this, it
was his mode of arriving at them. He introduced into
morals and politics those habits of thought and modes
of investigation, which are essential to the idea of
science; and the absence of which made those depart-
ments of inquiry, as physics had been before Bacon,
a field of interminable discussion, leading to no result.
It was not his opinions, in short, but his method, that
constituted the novelty and the value of what he did;
a value beyond all price, even though we should reject
the whole, as we unquestionably must a large part, of
the opinions themselves.

Bentham's method may be shortly described as the
method of detail; of treating wholes by separating
them into their parts, abstractions by resolving them
into Things,—classes and generalities by distinguish-
ing them into the individuals of which they are made
up; and breaking every question into pieces before
attempting to solve it. The precise amount of originality of this process, considered as a logical conception
—its degree of connexion with the methods of physical
science, or with the previous labours of Bacon, Hobbes,
or Locke—is not an essential consideration in this
place. Whatever originality there was in the method
—in the subjects he applied it to, and in the rigidity
with which he adhered to it, there was the greatest.
Hence his interminable classifications. Hence his
elaborate demonstrations of the most acknowledged
truths. That murder, incendiarism, robbery, are mischievous actions, he will not take for granted without
proof; let the thing appear ever so self-evident, he will

expressing facts, and that the only practical mode of
dealing with them is to trace them back to the facts
(whether of experience or of consciousness) of which
they are the expression. Proceeding on this principle,
Bentham makes short work with the ordinary modes
of moral and political reasoning. These, it appeared to
him, when hunted to their source, for the most part
terminated in *phrases*. In politics, liberty, social order,
constitution, law of nature, social compact, &c. were
the catchwords: ethics had its analogous ones. Such
were the arguments on which the gravest questions of
morality and policy were made to turn; not reasons,
but allusions to reasons; sacramental expressions, by
which a summary appeal was made to some general
sentiment of mankind, or to some maxim in familiar
use, which might be true or not, but the limitations of
which no one had ever critically examined. And this
satisfied other people; but not Bentham. He required
something more than opinion as a reason for opinion.
Whenever he found a *phrase* used as an argument for
or against anything, he insisted upon knowing what
it meant; whether it appealed to any standard, or gave
intimation of any matter of fact relevant to the question; and if he could not find that it did either, he
treated it as an attempt on the part of the disputant
to impose his own individual sentiment on other people,
without giving them a reason for it; a 'contrivance for
avoiding the obligation of appealing to any external
standard, and for prevailing upon the reader to accept
of the author's sentiment and opinion as a reason, and
that a sufficient one, for itself.' Bentham shall speak
for himself on this subject: the passage is from his
first systematic work, 'Introduction to the Principles
of Morals and Legislation,' and we could scarcely quote

anything more strongly exemplifying both the strength
and weakness of his mode of philosophizing.

'It is curious enough to observe the variety of inven-
tions men have hit upon, and the variety of phrases they
have brought forward, in order to conceal from the
world, and, if possible, from themselves, this very
general and therefore very pardonable self-sufficiency.

'1. One man says, he has a thing made on purpose to
tell him what is right and what is wrong; and that is
called a 'moral sense:' and then he goes to work at his
ease, and says, such a thing is right, and such a thing is
wrong—why? 'Because my moral sense tells me it is.'

'2. Another man comes and alters the phrase: leaving
out *moral*, and putting in *common* in the room of it. He
then tells you that his common sense tells him what is
right and wrong, as surely as the other's moral sense
did: meaning by common sense a sense of some kind or
other, which, he says, is possessed by all mankind: the
sense of those whose sense is not the same as the author's
being struck out as not worth taking. This contrivance
does better than the other; for a moral sense being a
new thing, a man may feel about him a good while
without being able to find it out: but common sense is
as old as the creation; and there is no man but would be
ashamed to be thought not to have as much of it as his
neighbours. It has another great advantage: by appear-
ing to share power, it lessens envy; for when a man gets
up upon this ground, in order to anathematize those who
differ from him, it is not by a *sic volo sic jubeo*, but by
a *velitis jubeatis*.

'3. Another man comes, and says, that as to a moral
sense indeed, he cannot find that he has any such thing:
that, however, he has an *understanding*, which will do
quite as well. This understanding, he says, is the
standard of right and wrong: it tells him so and so. All
good and wise men understand as he does: if other men's

understandings differ in any part from his, so much the worse for them: it is a sure sign they are either defective or corrupt.

'4. Another man says, that there is an eternal and immutable Rule of Right: that that rule of right dictates so and so: and then he begins giving you his sentiments upon anything that comes uppermost: and these sentiments (you are to take for granted) are so many branches of the eternal rule of right.

'5. Another man, or perhaps the same man (it is no matter), says that there are certain practices conformable, and others repugnant, to the Fitness of Things; and then he tells you, at his leisure, what practices are conformable, and what repugnant: just as he happens to like a practice or dislike it.

'6. A great multitude of people are continually talking of the Law of Nature; and then they go on giving you their sentiments about what is right and what is wrong: and these sentiments, you are to understand, are so many chapters and sections of the Law of Nature.

'7. Instead of the phrase, Law of Nature, you have sometimes Law of Reason, Right Reason, Natural Justice, Natural Equity, Good Order. Any of them will do equally well. This latter is most used in politics. The three last are much more tolerable than the others, because they do not very explicitly claim to be anything more than phrases: they insist but feebly upon the being looked upon as so many positive standards of themselves, and seem content to be taken, upon occasion, for phrases expressive of the conformity of the thing in question to the proper standard, whatever that may be. On most occasions, however, it will be better to say *utility: utility* is clearer, as referring more explicitly to pain and pleasure.

'8. We have one philosopher, who says, there is no harm in anything in the world but in telling a lie; and that if, for example, you were to murder your own

would imply great ignorance of the history of philosophy, of general literature, and of Bentham's own
writings. He derived the idea, as he says himself, from
Helvetius; and it was the doctrine no less, of the
religious philosophers of that age, prior to Reid and
Beattie. We never saw an abler defence of the doctrine
of utility than in a book written in refutation of
Shaftesbury, and now little read—Brown's[1] 'Essays
on the Characteristics'; and in Johnson's celebrated
review of Soame Jenyns, the same doctrine is set forth
as that both of the author and of the reviewer. In all
ages of philosophy one of its schools has been utilitarian
—not only from the time of Epicurus, but long before.
It was by mere accident that this opinion became
connected in Bentham with his peculiar method. The
utilitarian philosophers antecedent to him had no
more claims to the method than their antagonists.
To refer, for instance, to the Epicurean philosophy,
according to the most complete view we have of the
moral part of it, by the most accomplished scholar of
antiquity, Cicero; we ask any one who has read his
philosophical writings, the 'De Finibus' for instance,
whether the arguments of the Epicureans do not, just
as much as those of the Stoics or Platonists, consist of
mere rhetorical appeals to common notions, to εἰκότα
and σημεῖα instead of τεκμήρια, notions picked up as
it were casually, and when true at all, never so
narrowly looked into as to ascertain in what sense and
under what limitations they are true. The application
of a real inductive philosophy to the problems of ethics,
is as unknown to the Epicurean moralists as to any of
the other schools; they never take a question to pieces,

[1] Author of another book which made no little sensation when it
first appeared,—'An Estimate of the Manners of the Times.'

use of a method right in itself, and not adopted by his predecessors; it cannot be but that Bentham by his own inquiries must have accomplished something considerable. And so, it will be found, he has; something not only considerable, but extraordinary; though but little compared with what he has left undone, and far short of what his sanguine and almost boyish fancy made him flatter himself that he had accomplished. His peculiar method, admirably calculated to make clear thinkers, and sure ones to the extent of their materials, has not equal efficacy for making those materials complete. It is a security for accuracy, but not for comprehensiveness; or rather, it is a security for one sort of comprehensiveness, but not for another.

Bentham's method of laying out his subject is admirable as a preservative against one kind of narrow and partial views. He begins by placing before himself the whole of the field of inquiry to which the particular question belongs, and divides down till he arrives at the thing he is in search of; and thus by successively rejecting all which is *not* the thing, he gradually works out a definition of what it *is*. This, which he calls the exhaustive method, is as old as philosophy itself. Plato owes everything to it, and does everything by it; and the use made of it by that great man in his Dialogues, Bacon, in one of those pregnant logical hints scattered through his writings, and so much neglected by most of his pretended followers, pronounces to be the nearest approach to a true inductive method in the ancient philosophy. Bentham was probably not aware that Plato had anticipated him in the process to which he too declared that he owed everything. By the practice of it, his speculations are rendered eminently systematic and consistent; no question, with him, is ever an insulated one; he sees every subject in connexion with all the other subjects with which in his view it is related, and from which it requires to be distinguished; and as all that he knows, in the least degree allied to the subject, has been marshalled in an orderly manner before him, he does not, like people who use a looser method, forget and overlook a thing on one occasion to remember it on another. Hence there is probably no philosopher of so wide a range, in whom there are so few inconsistencies. If any of the truths which he did not see, had come to be seen by him, he would have remembered it everywhere and at all times, and would have adjusted his whole system to it. And this is another admirable quality which he has impressed upon the best of the minds trained in his habits of thought: when those minds open to admit new truths, they digest them as fast as they receive them.

But this system, excellent for keeping before the mind of the thinker all that he knows, does not make him know enough; it does not make a knowledge of some of the properties of a thing suffice for the whole of it, nor render a rooted habit of surveying a complex object (though ever so carefully) in only one of its aspects, tantamount to the power of contemplating it in all. To give this last power, other qualities are required: whether Bentham possessed those other qualities we now have to see.

Bentham's mind, as we have already said, was eminently synthetical. He begins all his inquiries by supposing nothing to be known on the subject, and reconstructs all philosophy *ab initio*, without reference to the opinions of his predecessors. But to build either a philosophy or anything else, there must be materials. For the philosophy of matter, the materials are the properties of matter; for moral and political philosophy, the properties of man, and of man's position in the world. The knowledge which any inquirer possesses of these properties, constitutes a limit beyond which, as a moralist or a political philosopher, whatever be his powers of mind, he cannot reach. Nobody's synthesis can be more complete than his analysis. If in his survey of human nature and life he has left any element out, then, wheresoever that element exerts any influence, his conclusions will fail, more or less, in their application. If he has left out many elements, and those very important, his labours may be highly valuable; he may have largely contributed to that body of partial truths which, when completed and corrected by one another, constitute practical truth; but the applicability of his system to practice in its own proper shape will be of an exceedingly limited range.

Human nature and human life are wide subjects, and whoever would embark in an enterprise requiring a thorough knowledge of them, has need both of large stores of his own, and of all aids and appliances from elsewhere. His qualifications for success will be proportional to two things: the degree in which his own nature and circumstances furnish him with a correct and complete picture of man's nature and circumstances; and his capacity of deriving light from other minds.

Bentham failed in deriving light from other minds. His writings contain few traces of the accurate knowledge of any schools of thinking but his own; and many proofs of his entire conviction that they could teach him nothing worth knowing. For some of the most illustrious of previous thinkers, his contempt was unmeasured. In almost the only passage of the 'Deonto-

logy' which, from its style, and from its having before
appeared in print, may be known to be Bentham's,
Socrates and Plato are spoken of in terms distressing
to his greatest admirers; and the incapacity to appreciate such men, is a fact perfectly in unison with the
general habits of Bentham's mind. He had a phrase,
expressive of the view he took of all moral speculations
to which his method had not been applied, or (which he
considered as the same thing) not founded on a recognition of utility as the moral standard; this phrase was
'vague generalities'. Whatever presented itself to him
in such a shape, he dismissed as unworthy of notice, or
dwelt upon only to denounce as absurd. He did not
heed, or rather the nature of his mind prevented it
from occurring to him, that these generalities contained the whole unanalysed experience of the human
race.

Unless it can be asserted that mankind did not know
anything until logicians taught it to them—that until
the last hand has been put to a moral truth by giving
it a metaphysically precise expression, all the previous
rough-hewing which it has undergone by the common
intellect at the suggestion of common wants and common experience is to go for nothing; it must be allowed,
that even the originality which can, and the courage
which dares, think for itself, is not a more necessary
part of the philosophical character than a thoughtful
regard for previous thinkers, and for the collective
mind of the human race. What has been the opinion
of mankind, has been the opinion of persons of all
tempers and dispositions, of all partialities and pre-
possessions, of all varieties in position, in education, in
opportunities of observation and inquiry. No one inquirer is all this; every inquirer is either young or old,

rich or poor, sickly or healthy, married or unmarried, meditative or active, a poet or a logician, an ancient or a modern, a man or a woman; and if a thinking person, has, in addition, the accidental peculiarities of his individual modes of thought. Every circumstance which gives a character to the life of a human being, carries with it its peculiar biasses; its peculiar facilities for perceiving some things, and for missing or forgetting others. But, from points of view different from his, different things are perceptible; and none are more likely to have seen what he does not see, than those who do not see what he sees. The general opinion of mankind is the average of the conclusions of all minds, stripped indeed of their choicest and most recondite thoughts, but freed from their twists and partialities: a net result, in which everybody's particular point of view is represented, nobody's predominant. The collective mind does not penetrate below the surface, but it sees all the surface; which profound thinkers, even by reason of their profundity, often fail to do: their intenser view of a thing in some of its aspects diverting their attention from others.

The hardiest assertor, therefore, of the freedom of private judgment—the keenest detector of the errors of his predecessors, and of the inaccuracies of current modes of thought—is the very person who most needs to fortify the weak side of his own intellect, by study of the opinions of mankind in all ages and nations, and of the speculations of philosophers of the modes of thought most opposite to his own. It is there that he will find the experiences denied to himself—the remainder of the truth of which he sees but half—the truths, of which the errors he detects are commonly but the exaggerations. If, like Bentham, he brings with him an improved instrument of investigation, the greater is the probability that he will find ready prepared a rich abundance of rough ore, which was merely waiting for that instrument. A man of clear ideas errs grievously if he imagines that whatever is seen confusedly does not exist: it belongs to him, when he meets with such a thing, to dispel the mist, and fix the outlines of the vague form which is looming through it.

Bentham's contempt, then, of all other schools of thinkers; his determination to create a philosophy wholly out of the materials furnished by his own mind, and by minds like his own; was his first disqualification as a philosopher. His second, was the incompleteness of his own mind as a representative of universal human nature. In many of the most natural and strongest feelings of human nature he had no sympathy; from many of its graver experiences he was altogether cut off; and the faculty by which one mind understands a mind different from itself, and throws itself into the feelings of that other mind, was denied him by his deficiency of Imagination.

With Imagination in the popular sense, command of imagery and metaphorical expression, Bentham was, to a certain degree, endowed. For want, indeed, of poetical culture, the images with which his fancy supplied him were seldom beautiful, but they were quaint and humorous, or bold, forcible, and intense: passages might be quoted from him both of playful irony, and of declamatory eloquence, seldom surpassed in the writings of philosophers. The Imagination which he had not, was that to which the name is generally appropriated by the best writers of the present day; that which enables us, by a voluntary effort, to

61

conceive the absent as if it were present, the imaginary as if it were real, and to clothe it in the feelings which, if it were indeed real, it would bring along with it. This is the power by which one human being enters into the mind and circumstances of another. This power constitutes the poet, in so far as he does anything but melodiously utter his own actual feelings. It constitutes the dramatist entirely. It is one of the constituents of the historian; by it we understand other times; by it Guizot interprets to us the middle ages; Nisard, in his beautiful Studies on the later Latin poets, places us in the Rome of the Cæsars; Michelet disengages the distinctive characters of the different races and generations of mankind from the facts of their history. Without it nobody knows even his own nature, further than circumstances have actually tried it and called it out; nor the nature of his fellow-creatures, beyond such generalizations as he may have been enabled to make from his observation of their outward conduct.

By these limits, accordingly, Bentham's knowledge of human nature is bounded. It is wholly empirical; and the empiricism of one who has had little experience. He had neither internal experience nor external; the quiet, even tenor of his life, and his healthiness of mind, conspired to exclude him from both. He never knew prosperity and adversity, passion nor satiety: he never had even the experiences which sickness gives; he lived from childhood to the age of eighty-five in boyish health. He knew no dejection, no heaviness of heart. He never felt life a sore and a weary burthen. He was a boy to the last. Self-consciousness, that dæmon of the men of genius of our time, from Wordsworth to Byron, from Goethe to Chateaubriand, and to which this age owes so much both of its cheerful and its mournful wisdom, never was awakened in him. How much of human nature slumbered in him he knew not, neither can we know. He had never been made alive to the unseen influences which were acting on himself, nor consequently on his fellow-creatures. Other ages and other nations were a blank to him for purposes of instruction. He measured them but by one standard; their knowledge of facts, and their capability to take correct views of utility, and merge all other objects in it. His own lot was cast in a generation of the leanest and barrenest men whom England had yet produced, and he was an old man when a better race came in with the present century. He saw accordingly in man little but what the vulgarest eye can see; recognised no diversities of character but such as he who runs may read. Knowing so little of human feelings, he knew still less of the influences by which those feelings are formed: all the more subtle workings both of the mind upon itself, and of external things upon the mind, escaped him; and no one, probably, who, in a highly instructed age, ever attempted to give a rule to all human conduct, set out with a more limited conception either of the agencies by which human conduct *is*, or of those by which it *should* be, influenced.

This, then, is our idea of Bentham. He was a man both of remarkable endowments for philosophy, and of remarkable deficiencies for it: fitted, beyond almost any man, for drawing from his premises, conclusions not only correct, but sufficiently precise and specific to be practical: but whose general conception of human nature and life, furnished him with an unusually slender stock of premises. It is obvious what would be likely to be achieved by such a man; what a thinker, thus gifted and thus disqualified, could do in philosophy. He could, with close and accurate logic, hunt half-truths to their consequences and practical applications, on a scale both of greatness and of minuteness not previously exemplified; and this is the character which posterity will probably assign to Bentham.

We express our sincere and well-considered conviction when we say, that there is hardly anything positive in Bentham's philosophy which is not true: that when his practical conclusions are erroneous, which in our opinion they are very often, it is not because the considerations which he urges are not rational and valid in themselves, but because some more important principle, which he did not perceive, supersedes those considerations, and turns the scale. The bad part of his writings is his resolute denial of all that he does not see, of all truths but those which he recognises. By that alone has he exercised any bad influence upon his age; by that he has, not created a school of deniers, for this is an ignorant prejudice, but put himself at the head of the school which exists always, though it does not always find a great man to give it the sanction of philosophy: thrown the mantle of intellect over the natural tendency of men in all ages to deny or disparage all feelings and mental states of which they have no consciousness in themselves.

The truths which are not Bentham's, which his philosophy takes no account of, are many and important; but his non-recognition of them does not put them out of existence; they are still with us, and it is a comparatively easy task that is reserved for us, to harmonize those truths with his. To reject his half of the truth because he overlooked the other half, would be to fall into his error without having his excuse. For our own part, we have a large tolerance for one-eyed men, provided their one eye is a penetrating one: if they saw more, they probably would not see so keenly, nor so eagerly pursue one course of inquiry. Almost all rich veins of original and striking specula-tion have been opened by systematic half-thinkers: though whether these new thoughts drive out others as good, or are peacefully superadded to them, depends on whether these half-thinkers are or are not followed in the same track by complete thinkers. The field of man's nature and life cannot be too much worked, or in too many directions; until every clod is turned up the work is imperfect; no whole truth is possible but by combining the points of view of all the fractional truths, nor, therefore, until it has been fully seen what each fractional truth can do by itself.

What Bentham's fractional truths could do, there is no such good means of showing as by a review of his philosophy: and such a review, though inevitably a most brief and general one, it is now necessary to attempt.

The first question in regard to any man of specula-tion is, what is his theory of human life? In the minds of many philosophers, whatever theory they have of this sort is latent, and it would be a revelation to themselves to have it pointed out to them in their writings as others can see it, unconsciously moulding everything to its own likeness. But Bentham always knew his own premises, and made his reader know them: it was not his custom to leave the theoretic grounds of his practical conclusions to conjecture. Few great thinkers have afforded the means of assigning with so much certainty the exact conception which they had formed of man and of man's life.

Man is conceived by Bentham as a being susceptible of pleasures and pains, and governed in all his conduct partly by the different modifications of self-interest, and the passions commonly classed as selfish, partly by sympathies, or occasionally antipathies, towards other beings. And here Bentham's conception of human nature stops. He does not exclude religion; the prospect of divine rewards and punishments he includes under the head of 'self-regarding interest,' and the devotional feeling under that of sympathy with God. But the whole of the impelling or restraining principles, whether of this or of another world, which he recognises, are either self-love, or love or hatred towards other sentient beings. That there might be no doubt of what he thought on the subject, he has not left us to the general evidence of his writings, but has drawn out a 'Table of the Springs of Action,' an express enumeration and classification of human motives, with their various names, laudatory, vituperative, and neutral: and this table, to be found in Part I. of his collected works, we recommend to the study of those who would understand his philosophy.

Man is never recognised by him as a being capable of pursuing spiritual perfection as an end; of desiring, for its own sake, the conformity of his own character to his standard of excellence, without hope of good or fear of evil from other source than his own inward consciousness. Even in the more limited form of Conscience, this great fact in human nature escapes him. Nothing is more curious than the absence of recognition in any of his writings of the existence of conscience, as a thing distinct from philanthropy, from affection for God or man, and from self-interest in this world or in the next. There is a studied abstinence from any of the phrases which, in the mouths of others, import the acknowledgment of such a fact.[1] If we find the words 'Conscience', 'Principle', 'Moral Rectitude', 'Moral Duty', in his Table of the Springs of Action, it is among the synonymes of the 'love of reputation'; with an intimation as to the two former phrases, that they are also sometimes synonymous with the *religious* motive, or the motive of *sympathy*. The feeling of moral approbation or disapprobation properly so called, either towards ourselves or our fellow-creatures, he seems unaware of the existence of; and neither the word *self-respect*, nor the idea to which that word is appropriated, occurs even once, so far as our recollection serves us, in his whole writings.

Nor is it only the moral part of man's nature, in the strict sense of the term—the desire of perfection, or the feeling of an approving or of an accusing conscience—that he overlooks; he but faintly recognises, as a fact in human nature, the pursuit of any other ideal end for its own sake. The sense of *honour*, and personal dignity—that feeling of personal exaltation and degradation which acts independently of other people's opinion, or even in defiance of it; the love of *beauty*, the passion of the artist; the love of *order*, of congruity, of consistency in all things, and conformity to their end; the love of *power*, not in the limited form of power over other human beings, but abstract power, the power of making our volitions effectual; the love of *action*, the thirst for movement and activity,

[1] In a passage in the last volume of his book on Evidence, and possibly in one or two other places, the 'love of justice' is spoken of as a feeling inherent in almost all mankind. It is impossible, without explanations now unattainable, to ascertain what sense is to be put upon casual expressions so inconsistent with the general tenor of his philosophy.

a principle scarcely of less influence in human life than its opposite, the love of ease:—None of these powerful constituents of human nature are thought worthy of a place among the 'Springs of Action;' and though there is possibly no one of them of the existence of which an acknowledgment might not be found in some corner of Bentham's writings, no conclusions are ever founded on the acknowledgment. Man, that most complex being, is a very simple one in his eyes. Even under the head of *sympathy*, his recognition does not extend to the more complex forms of the feeling—the love of *loving*, the need of a sympathising support, or of objects of admiration and reverence. If he thought at all of any of the deeper feelings of human nature, it was but as idiosyncrasies of taste, with which the moralist no more than the legislator had any concern, further than to prohibit such as were mischievous among the actions to which they might chance to lead. To say either that man should, or that he should not, take pleasure in one thing, displeasure in another, appeared to him as much an act of despotism in the moralist as in the political ruler.

It would be most unjust to Bentham to surmise (as narrow-minded and passionate adversaries are apt in such cases to do) that this picture of human nature was copied from himself; that all those constituents of humanity which he rejected from his table of motives, were wanting in his own breast. The unusual strength of his early feelings of virtue, was, as we have seen, the original cause of all his speculations; and a noble sense of morality, and especially of justice, guides and pervades them all. But having been early accustomed to keep before his mind's eye the happiness of mankind (or rather of the whole sentient world), as the only thing desirable in itself, or which rendered anything else desirable, he confounded all disinterested feelings which he found in himself, with the desire of general happiness: just as some religious writers, who loved virtue for its own sake as much perhaps as men could do, habitually confounded their love of virtue with their fear of hell. It would have required greater subtlety than Bentham possessed, to distinguish from each other, feelings which, from long habit, always acted in the same direction; and his want of imagination prevented him from reading the distinction, where it is legible enough, in the hearts of others.

Accordingly, he has not been followed in this grand oversight by any of the able men who, from the extent of their intellectual obligations to him, have been regarded as his disciples. They may have followed him in his doctrine of utility, and in his rejection of a moral sense as the test of right and wrong: but while repudiating it as such, they have, with Hartley, acknowledged it as a fact in human nature; they have endeavoured to account for it, to assign its laws: nor are they justly chargeable either with undervaluing this part of our nature, or with any disposition to throw it into the background of their speculations. If any part of the influence of this cardinal error has extended itself to them, it is circuitously, and through the effect on their minds of other parts of Bentham's doctrines.

Sympathy, the only disinterested motive which Bentham recognised, he felt the inadequacy of, except in certain limited cases, as a security for virtuous action. Personal affection, he well knew, is as liable to operate to the injury of third parties, and requires as much to be kept under government, as any other feeling whatever: and general philanthropy, considered as a motive influencing mankind in general, he estimated at its true value when divorced from the feeling of duty—as the very weakest and most unsteady of all feelings. There remained, as a motive by which mankind are influenced, and by which they may be guided to their good, only personal interest. Accordingly, Bentham's idea of the world is that of a collection of persons pursuing each his separate interest or pleasure, and the prevention of whom from jostling one another more than is unavoidable, may be attempted by hopes and fears derived from three sources—the law, religion, and public opinion. To these three powers, considered as binding human conduct, he gave the name of *sanctions*: the *political* sanction, operating by the rewards and penalties of the law; the *religious* sanction, by those expected from the Ruler of the Universe; and the *popular*, which he characteristically calls also the *moral* sanction, operating through the pains and pleasures arising from the favour or disfavour of our fellow-creatures.

Such is Bentham's theory of the world. And now, in a spirit neither of apology nor of censure, but of calm appreciation, we are to inquire how far this view of human nature and life will carry any one:—how much it will accomplish in morals, and how much in political and social philosophy: what it will do for the individual, and what for society.

It will do nothing for the conduct of the individual, beyond prescribing some of the more obvious dictates of worldly prudence, and outward probity and beneficence. There is no need to expatiate on the deficiencies of a system of ethics which does not pretend to aid individuals in the formation of their own character;

which recognises no such wish as that of self-culture, we may even say no such power, as existing in human nature; and if it did recognise, could furnish little assistance to that great duty, because it overlooks the existence of about half of the whole number of mental feelings which human beings are capable of, including all those of which the direct objects are states of their own mind.

Morality consists of two parts. One of these is self-education; the training, by the human being himself, of his affections and will. That department is a blank in Bentham's system. The other and co-equal part, the regulation of his outward actions, must be altogether halting and imperfect without the first: for how can we judge in what manner many an action will affect even the worldly interests of ourselves or others, unless we take in, as part of the question, its influence on the regulation of our, or their, affections and desires? A moralist on Bentham's principles may get as far as this, that he ought not to slay, burn, or steal; but what will be his qualifications for regulating the nicer shades of human behaviour, or for laying down even the greater moralities as to those facts in human life which are liable to influence the depths of the character quite independently of any influence on worldly circumstances—such, for instance, as the sexual relations, or those of family in general, or any other social and sympathetic connexions of an intimate kind? The moralities of these questions depend essentially on considerations which Bentham never so much as took into the account; and when he happened to be in the right, it was always, and necessarily, on wrong or insufficient grounds.

It is fortunate for the world that Bentham's taste

lay rather in the direction of jurisprudential than of properly ethical inquiry. Nothing expressly of the latter kind has been published under his name, except the 'Deontology'—a book scarcely ever, in our experience, alluded to by any admirer of Bentham without deep regret that it ever saw the light. We did not expect from Bentham correct systematic views of ethics, or a sound treatment of any question the moralities of which require a profound knowledge of the human heart; but we did anticipate that the greater moral questions would have been boldly plunged into, and at least a searching criticism produced of the received opinions; we did not expect that the *petite morale* almost alone would have been treated, and that with the most pedantic minuteness, and on the *quid pro quo* principles which regulate trade. The book has not even the value which would belong to an authentic exhibition of the legitimate consequences of an erroneous line of thought; for the style proves it to have been so entirely rewritten, that it is impossible to tell how much or how little of it is Bentham's. The collected edition, now in progress, will not, it is said, include Bentham's religious writings; these, although we think most of them of exceedingly small value, are at least his, and the world has a right to whatever light they throw upon the constitution of his mind. But the omission of the 'Deontology' would be an act of editorial discretion which we should deem entirely justifiable.

If Bentham's theory of life can do so little for the individual, what can it do for society?

It will enable a society which has attained a certain state of spiritual development, and the maintenance of which in that state is otherwise provided for, to prescribe the rules by which it may protect its material interests. It will do nothing (except sometimes as an instrument in the hands of a higher doctrine) for the spiritual interests of society; nor does it suffice of itself even for the material interests. That which alone causes any material interests to exist, which alone enables any body of human beings to exist as a society, is national character: *that* it is, which causes one nation to succeed in what it attempts, another to fail; one nation to understand and aspire to elevated things, another to grovel in mean ones; which makes the greatness of one nation lasting, and dooms another to early and rapid decay. The true teacher of the fitting social arrangements for England, France, or America, is the one who can point out how the English, French, or American character can be improved, and how it has been made what it is. A philosophy of laws and institutions, not founded on a philosophy of national character, is an absurdity. But what could Bentham's opinion be worth on national character? How could he, whose mind contained so few and so poor types of individual character, rise to that higher generalization? All he can do is but to indicate means by which, in any given state of the national mind, the material interests of society can be protected; saving the question, of which others must judge, whether the use of those means would have, on the national character, any injurious influence.

We have arrived, then, at a sort of estimate of what a philosophy like Bentham's can do. It can teach the means of organizing and regulating the merely *business* part of the social arrangements. Whatever can be understood or whatever done without reference to moral influences, his philosophy is equal to; where those influences require to be taken into account, it is at fault. He committed the mistake of supposing that the business part of human affairs was the whole of them; all at least that the legislator and the moralist had to do with. Not that he disregarded moral influences when he perceived them; but his want of imagination, small experience of human feelings, and ignorance of the filiation and connexion of feelings with one another, made this rarely the case.

The business part is accordingly the only province of human affairs which Bentham has cultivated with any success; into which he has introduced any considerable number of comprehensive and luminous practical principles. That is the field of his greatness; and there he is indeed great. He has swept away the accumulated cobwebs of centuries—he has untied knots which the efforts of the ablest thinkers, age after age, had only drawn tighter; and it is no exaggeration to say of him that over a great part of the field he was the first to shed the light of reason.

We turn with pleasure from what Bentham could not do, to what he did. It is an ungracious task to call a great benefactor of mankind to account for not being a greater—to insist upon the errors of a man who has originated more new truths, has given to the world more sound practical lessons, than it ever received, except in a few glorious instances, from any other individual. The unpleasing part of our work is ended. We are now to show the greatness of the man; the grasp which his intellect took of the subjects with which it was fitted to deal; the giant's task which was before him, and the hero's courage and strength with which he achieved it. Nor let that which he did be deemed of small account because its province was

unless something had been done to adapt those laws to it. But the adaptation was not the result of thought and design; it arose not from any comprehensive consideration of the new state of society and its exigencies. What was done, was done by a struggle of centuries between the old barbarism and the new civilization; between the feudal aristocracy of conquerors, holding fast to the rude system they had established, and the conquered effecting their emancipation. The last was the growing power, but was never strong enough to break its bonds, though ever and anon some weak point gave way. Hence the law came to be like the costume of a full-grown man who had never put off the clothes made for him when he first went to school. Band after band had burst, and, as the rent widened, then, without removing anything except what might drop off of itself, the hole was darned, or patches of fresh law were brought from the nearest shop and stuck on. Hence all ages of English history have given one another rendezvous in English law; their several products may be seen all together, not interfused, but heaped one upon another, as many different ages of the earth may be read in some perpendicular section of its surface—the deposits of each successive period not substituted but superimposed on those of the preceding. And in the world of law no less than in the physical world, every commotion and conflict of the elements has left its mark behind in some break or irregularity of the strata: every struggle which ever rent the bosom of society is apparent in the disjointed condition of the part of the field of law which covers the spot: nay, the very traps and pitfalls which one contending party set for another are still standing, and the teeth not of hyenas only, but of foxes and all cunning animals, are imprinted on the curious remains found in these antediluvian caves.

In the English law, as in the Roman before it, the adaptations of barbarous laws to the growth of civilized society were made chiefly by stealth. They were generally made by the courts of justice, who could not help reading the new wants of mankind in the cases between man and man which came before them; but who, having no authority to make new laws for those new wants, were obliged to do the work covertly, and evade the jealousy and opposition of an ignorant, prejudiced, and for the most part brutal and tyrannical legislature. Some of the most necessary of these improvements, such as the giving force of law to trusts, and the breaking up of entails, were effected in actual opposition to the strongly-declared will of Parliament, whose clumsy hands, no match for the astuteness of judges, could not, after repeated trials, manage to make any law which the judges could not find a trick for rendering inoperative. The whole history of the contest about trusts may still be read in the words of a conveyance, as could the contest about entails, till the abolition of fine and recovery by a bill of the present Attorney-General; but dearly did the client pay for the cabinet of historical curiosities which he was obliged to purchase every time that he made a settlement of his estate. The result of this mode of improving social institutions was, that whatever new things were done had to be done in consistency with old forms and names; and the laws were improved with much the same effect as if, in the improvement of agriculture, the plough could only have been introduced by making it look like a spade; or as if, when the primeval practice of ploughing by the horse's tail gave way to the innovation of harness, the tail, for form's sake, had still remained attached to the plough.

When the conflicts were over, and the mixed mass settled down into something like a fixed state, and that state a very profitable and therefore a very agreeable one to lawyers, they, following the natural tendency of the human mind, began to theorise upon it, and, in obedience to necessity, had to digest it and give it a systematic form. It was from this thing of shreds and patches, in which the only part that approached to order or system was the early barbarous part, already more than half superseded, that English lawyers had to construct, by induction and abstraction, their philosophy of law; and without the logical habits and general intellectual cultivation which the lawyers of the Roman empire brought to a similar task. Bentham found the philosophy of law what English practising lawyers had made it; a jumble, in which *real* and *personal* property, *law* and *equity*, *felony*, *premunire*, *misprision*, and *misdemeanour*, words without a vestige of meaning when detached from the history of English institutions—mere tide-marks to point out the line which the sea and the shore, in their secular struggles, had adjusted as their mutual boundary—all passed for distinctions inherent in the nature of things; in which every absurdity, every lucrative abuse, had a reason found for it—a reason which only now and then even pretended to be drawn from expediency; most commonly a technical reason, one of mere form, derived from the old barbarous system. While the theory of the law was in this state, to describe what the practice of it was would require the pen of a Swift, or of Bentham himself. The whole progress of a suit at law seemed like a series of contrivances for lawyers' profit, in which the suitors were regarded as the prey; and if the poor were not the helpless victims of every Sir Giles Overreach who could pay the price, they might thank opinion and manners for it, not the law.

It may be fancied by some people that Bentham did an easy thing in merely calling all this absurd, and proving it to be so. But he began the contest a young man, and he had grown old before he had any followers. History will one day refuse to give credit to the intensity of the superstition which, till very lately, protected this mischievous mess from examination or doubt—passed off the charming representations of Blackstone for a just estimate of the English law, and proclaimed the shame of human reason to be the perfection of it. Glory to Bentham that he has dealt to this superstition its deathblow—that he has been the Hercules of this hydra, the St. George of this pestilent dragon! The honour is all his—nothing but his peculiar qualities could have done it. There were wanted his indefatigable perseverance, his firm self-reliance, needing no support from other men's opinion; his intensely practical turn of mind, his synthetical habits—above all, his peculiar method. Metaphysicians, armed with vague generalities, had often tried their hands at the subject, and left it no more advanced than they found it. Law is a matter of business; means and ends are the things to be considered in it, not abstractions: vagueness was not to be met by vagueness, but by definiteness and precision: details were not to be encountered with generalities, but with details. Nor could any progress be made, on such a subject, by merely showing that existing things were bad; it was necessary also to show how they might be made better. No great man whom we read of was qualified to do this thing except Bentham. He has done it, once and for ever.

Into the particulars of what Bentham has done we cannot enter: many hundred pages would be required to give a tolerable abstract of it. To sum up our estimate under a few heads. First: he has expelled mysticism from the philosophy of law, and set the example of viewing laws in a practical light, as means to certain definite and precise ends. Secondly: he has cleared up the confusion and vagueness attaching to the idea of law in general, to the idea of a body of laws, and all the general ideas therein involved. Thirdly: he demonstrated the necessity and practicability of *codification*, or the conversion of all law into a written and systematically arranged code: not like the Code Napoleon, a code without a single definition, requiring a constant reference to anterior precedent for the meaning of its technical terms; but one containing within itself all that is necessary for its own interpretation, together with a perpetual provision for its own emendation and improvement. He has shown of what parts such a code would consist; the relation of those parts to one another; and by his distinctions and classifications has done very much towards showing what should be, or might be, its nomenclature and arrangement. What he has left undone, he has made it comparatively easy for others to do. Fourthly: he has taken a systematic view[1] of the exigencies of society for which the civil code is intended to provide, and of the principles of human nature by which its provisions are to be tested: and this view, defective (as we have already intimated) wherever spiritual interests require

[1] See the 'Principles of Civil Law,' contained in Part II. of his collected works.

to be taken into account, is excellent for that large portion of the laws of any country which are designed for the protection of material interests. Fifthly: (to say nothing of the subject of punishment, for which something considerable had been done before) he found the philosophy of judicial procedure, including that of judicial establishments and of evidence, in a more wretched state than even any other part of the philosophy of law; he carried it at once almost to perfection. He left it with every one of its principles established, and little remaining to be done even in the suggestion of practical arrangements.

These assertions in behalf of Bentham may be left, without fear for the result, in the hands of those who are competent to judge of them. There are now even in the highest seats of justice, men to whom the claims made for him will not appear extravagant. Principle after principle of those propounded by him is moreover making its way by infiltration into the understandings most shut against his influence, and driving nonsense and prejudice from one corner of them to another. The reform of the laws of any country according to his principles, can only be gradual, and may be long ere it is accomplished; but the work is in progress, and both parliament and the judges are every year doing something, and often something not inconsiderable, towards the forwarding of it.

It seems proper here to take notice of an accusation sometimes made both against Bentham and against the principle of codification—as if they required one uniform suit of ready-made laws for all times and all states of society. The doctrine of codification, as the word imports, relates to the form only of the laws, not their substance; it does not concern itself with what

81

the laws should be, but declares that whatever they are, they ought to be systematically arranged, and fixed down to a determinate form of words. To the accusation, so far as it affects Bentham, one of the essays in the collection of his works (then for the first time published in English) is a complete answer: that 'On the Influence of Time and Place in Matters of Legislation.' It may there be seen that the different exigencies of different nations with respect to law, occupied his attention as systematically as any other portion of the wants which render laws necessary: with the limitations, it is true, which were set to all his speculations by the imperfections of his theory of human nature. For, taking, as we have seen, next to no account of national character and the causes which form and maintain it, he was precluded from considering, except to a very limited extent, the laws of a country as an instrument of national culture: one of their most important aspects, and in which they must of course vary according to the degree and kind of culture already attained; as a tutor gives his pupil different lessons according to the progress already made in his education. The same laws would not have suited our wild ancestors, accustomed to rude independence, and a people of Asiatics bowed down by military despotism: the slave needs to be trained to govern himself, the savage to submit to the government of others. The same laws will not suit the English, who distrust everything which emanates from general principles, and the French, who distrust whatever does not so emanate. Very different institutions are needed to train to the perfection of their nature, or to constitute into a united nation and social polity, an essentially *subjective* people like the Germans, and an essentially *objective* people like those of Northern and Central Italy; the one affectionate and dreamy, the other passionate and worldly; the one trustful and loyal, the other calculating and suspicious; the one not practical enough, the other overmuch; the one wanting individuality, the other fellow-feeling; the one failing for want of exacting enough for itself, the other for want of conceding enough to others. Bentham was little accustomed to look at institutions in their relation to these topics. The effects of this oversight must of course be perceptible throughout his speculations, but we do not think the errors into which it led him very material in the greater part of civil and penal law: it is in the department of constitutional legislation that they were fundamental.

The Benthamic theory of government has made so much noise in the world of late years; it has held such a conspicuous place among Radical philosophies, and Radical modes of thinking have participated so much more largely than any others in its spirit, that many worthy persons imagine there is no other Radical philosophy extant. Leaving such people to discover their mistake as they may, we shall expend a few words in attempting to discriminate between the truth and error of this celebrated theory.

There are three great questions in government. First, to what authority is it for the good of the people that they should be subject? Secondly, how are they to be induced to obey that authority? The answers to these two questions vary indefinitely, according to the degree and kind of civilization and cultivation already attained by a people, and their peculiar aptitudes for receiving more. Comes next a third question, not liable to so much variation, namely, by what means are the abuses of this authority to be checked? This third question is the only one of the three to which Bentham seriously applies himself, and he gives it the only answer it admits of—Responsibility: responsibility to persons whose interest, whose obvious and recognisable interest, accords with the end in view—good government. This being granted, it is next to be asked in what body of persons this identity of interest with good government, that is, with the interest of the whole community, is to be found? In nothing less, says Bentham, than the numerical majority: nor, say we, even in the numerical majority itself; of no portion of the community less than all, will the interest coincide, at all times and in all respects, with the interest of all. But, since power given to all, by a representative government, is in fact given to a majority; we are obliged to fall back upon the first of our three questions, namely, under what authority is it for the good of the people that they be placed? And if to this the answer be, under that of a majority among themselves, Bentham's system cannot be questioned. This one assumption being made, his 'Constitutional Code' is admirable. That extraordinary power which he possessed, of at once seizing comprehensive principles, and scheming out minute details, is brought into play with surpassing vigour in devising means for preventing rulers from escaping from the control of the majority; for enabling and inducing the majority to exercise that control unremittingly; and for providing them with servants of every desirable endowment, moral and intellectual, compatible with entire subservience to their will.

But *is* this fundamental doctrine of Bentham's political philosophy an universal truth? Is it, at all

times and places, good for mankind to be under the
absolute authority of the majority of themselves? We
say the authority, not the political authority merely,
because it is chimerical to suppose that whatever has
absolute power over men's bodies will not arrogate it
over their minds—will not seek to control (not perhaps
by legal penalties, but by the persecutions of society)
opinions and feelings which depart from its standard;
will not attempt to shape the education of the young
by its model, and to extinguish all 'books, all schools,
all combinations of individuals for joint action upon
society, which may be attempted for the purpose of
keeping alive a spirit at variance with its own. Is
it, we say, the proper condition of man, in all ages
and nations, to be under the despotism of Public
Opinion?

It is very conceivable that such a doctrine should
find acceptance from some of the noblest spirits, in a
time of reaction against the aristocratic governments
of modern Europe; governments founded on the entire
sacrifice (except so far as prudence, and sometimes
humane feeling interfere) of the community generally,
to the self-interest and ease of a few. European reformers have been accustomed to see the numerical
majority everywhere unjustly depressed, everywhere
trampled upon, or at the best overlooked, by governments; nowhere possessing power enough to extort
redress of their most positive grievances, provision for
their mental culture, or even to prevent themselves
from being taxed avowedly for the pecuniary profit
of the ruling classes. To see these things, and to seek
to put an end to them, by means (among other things)
of giving more political power to the majority, constitutes Radicalism; and it is because so many in this

age have felt this wish, and have felt that the realization of it was an object worthy of men's devoting their lives to it, that such a theory of government as Bentham's has found favour with them. But, though to pass from one form of bad government to another be the ordinary fate of mankind, philosophers ought not to make themselves parties to it, by sacrificing one portion of important truth to another.

The numerical majority of any society whatever, must consist of persons all standing in the same social position, and having, in the main, the same pursuits, namely, unskilled manual labourers; and we mean no disparagement to them: whatever we say to their disadvantage, we say equally of a numerical majority of shopkeepers, or of squires. Where there is identity of position and pursuits, there also will be identity of partialities, passions and prejudices; and to give to any one set of partialities, passions, and prejudices, absolute power, without counter-balance from partialities, passions, and prejudices of a different sort, is the way to render the correction of any of those imperfections hopeless; to make one narrow, mean type of human nature universal and perpetual, and to crush every influence which tends to the further improvement of man's intellectual and moral nature. There must, we know, be some paramount power in society; and that the majority should be that power, is on the whole right, not as being just in itself, but as being less unjust than any other footing on which the matter can be placed. But it is necessary that the institutions of society should make provision for keeping up, in some form or other, as a corrective to partial views, and a shelter for freedom of thought and individuality of character, a perpetual and standing Opposition to the will of the majority. All countries which have long continued progressive, or been durably great, have been so because there has been an organized opposition to the ruling power, of whatever kind that power was: plebeians to patricians, clergy to kings, freethinkers to clergy, kings to barons, commons to king and aristocracy. Almost all the greatest men who ever lived have formed part of such an Opposition. Wherever some such quarrel has not been going on—wherever it has been terminated by the complete victory of one of the contending principles, and no new contest has taken the place of the old—society has either hardened into Chinese stationariness, or fallen into dissolution. A centre of resistance, round which all the moral and social elements which the ruling power views with disfavour may cluster themselves, and behind whose bulwarks they may find shelter from the attempts of that power to hunt them out of existence, is as necessary where the opinion of the majority is sovereign, as where the ruling power is a hierarchy or an aristocracy. Where no such *point d'appui* exists, there the human race will inevitably degenerate; and the question, whether the United States, for instance, will in time sink into another China (also a most commercial and industrious nation), resolves itself, to us, into the question, whether such a centre of resistance will gradually evolve itself or not.

These things being considered, we cannot think that Bentham made the most useful employment which might have been made of his great powers, when, not content with enthroning the majority as sovereign, by means of universal suffrage without king or house of lords, he exhausted all the resources of ingenuity in devising means for riveting the yoke of public opinion closer and closer round the necks of all public functionaries, and excluding every possibility of the exercise of the slightest or most temporary influence either by a minority, or by the functionary's own notions of right. Surely when any power has been made the strongest power, enough has been done for it; care is thenceforth wanted rather to prevent that strongest power from swallowing up all others. Wherever all the forces of society act in one single direction, the just claims of the individual human being are in extreme peril. The power of the majority is salutary so far as it is used defensively, not offensively—as its exertion is tempered by respect for the personality of the individual, and deference to superiority of cultivated intelligence. If Bentham had employed himself in pointing out the means by which institutions fundamentally democratic might be best adapted to the preservation and strengthening of those two sentiments, he would have done something more permanently valuable, and more worthy of his great intellect. Montesquieu, with the lights of the present age, would have done it; and we are possibly destined to receive this benefit from the Montesquieu of our own times, M. de Tocqueville.

Do we then consider Bentham's political speculations useless? Far from it. We consider them only one-sided. He has brought out into a strong light, has cleared from a thousand confusions and misconceptions, and pointed out with admirable skill the best means of promoting, one of the ideal qualities of a perfect government—identity of interest between the trustees and the community for whom they hold their power in trust. This quality is not attainable in its ideal perfection, and must moreover be striven for with a perpetual eye to all other requisites; but those other requisites must still more be striven for without losing sight of this: and when the slightest postponement is made of it to any other end, the sacrifice, often necessary, is never unattended with evil. Bentham has pointed out how complete this sacrifice is in modern European societies: how exclusively, partial and sinister interests are the ruling power there, with only such check as is imposed by public opinion—which being thus, in the existing order of things, perpetually apparent as a source of good, he was led by natural partiality to exaggerate its intrinsic excellence. This sinister interest of rulers Bentham hunted through all its disguises, and especially through those which hide it from the men themselves who are influenced by it. The greatest service rendered by him to the philosophy of universal human nature, is, perhaps, his illustration of what he terms 'interest-begotten prejudice'—the common tendency of man to make a duty and a virtue of following his self-interest. The idea, it is true, was far from being peculiarly Bentham's: the artifices by which we persuade ourselves that we are not yielding to our selfish inclinations when we are, had attracted the notice of all moralists, and had been probed by religious writers to a depth as much below Bentham's, as their knowledge of the profundities and windings of the human heart was superior to his. But it is selfish interest in the form of class-interest, and the class morality founded thereon, which Bentham has illustrated: the manner in which any set of persons who mix much together, and have a common interest, are apt to make that common interest their standard of virtue, and the social feelings of the members of the class are made to play into the hands of their selfish ones; whence the union so often exemplified in history,

between the most heroic personal disinterestedness
and the most odious class-selfishness. This was one of
Bentham's leading ideas, and almost the only one by
which he contributed to the elucidation of history:
much of which, except so far as this explained it, must
have been entirely inexplicable to him. The idea was
given him by Helvetius, whose book, 'De l'Esprit', is
one continued and most acute commentary on it; and,
together with the other great idea of Helvetius, the
influence of circumstances on character, it will make
his name live by the side of Rousseau, when most of
the other French metaphysicians of the eighteenth
century will be extant as such only in literary history.

In the brief view which we have been able to give
of Bentham's philosophy, it may surprise the reader
that we have said so little about the first principle of
it, with which his name is more identified than with
anything else; the 'principle of utility', or, as he afterwards named it, 'the greatest-happiness principle.' It
is a topic on which much were to be said, if there were
room, or if it were in reality necessary for the just
estimation of Bentham. On an occasion more suitable
for a discussion of the metaphysics of morality, or on
which the elucidations necessary to make an opinion
on so abstract a subject intelligible could be conveniently given, we should be fully prepared to state
what we think on this subject. At present we shall only
say, that while, under proper explanations, we entirely
agree with Bentham in his principle, we do not hold
with him that all right thinking on the details of morals
depends on its express assertion. We think utility, or
happiness, much too complex and indefinite an end
to be sought except through the medium of various
secondary ends, concerning which there may be, and

often is, agreement among persons who differ in their ultimate standard; and about which there does in fact prevail a much greater unanimity among thinking persons, than might be supposed from their diametrical divergence on the great questions of moral metaphysics. As mankind are much more nearly of one nature, than of one opinion about their own nature, they are more easily brought to agree in their intermediate principles, *vera illa et media axiomata*, as Bacon says, than in their first principles: and the attempt to make the bearings of actions upon the ultimate end more evident than they can be made by referring them to the intermediate ends, and to estimate their value by a direct reference to human happiness, generally terminates in attaching most importance, not to those effects which are really the greatest, but to those which can most easily be pointed to and individually identified. Those who adopt utility as a standard can seldom apply it truly except through the secondary principles; those who reject it, generally do no more than erect those secondary principles into first principles. It is when two or more of the secondary principles conflict, that a direct appeal to some first principle becomes necessary; and then commences the practical importance of the utilitarian controversy; which is in other respects, a question of arrangement and logical subordination rather than of practice; important principally in a purely scientific point of view, for the sake of the systematic unity and coherency of ethical philosophy. It is probable, however, that to the principle of utility we owe all that Bentham did; that it was necessary to him to find a first principle which he could receive as self-evident, and to which he could attach all his other doctrines as logical consequences:

that to him systematic unity was an indispensable condition of his confidence in his own intellect. And there is something further to be remarked. Whether happiness be or be not the end to which morality should be referred—that it be referred to an *end* of some sort, and not left in the dominion of vague feeling or inexplicable internal conviction, that it be made a matter of reason and calculation, and not merely of sentiment, is essential to the very idea of moral philosophy; is, in fact, what renders argument or discussion on moral questions possible. That the morality of actions depends on the consequences which they tend to produce, is the doctrine of rational persons of all schools; that the good or evil of those consequences is measured solely by pleasure or pain, is all of the doctrine of the school of utility, which is peculiar to it.

In so far as Bentham's adoption of the principle of utility induced him to fix his attention upon the consequences of actions as the consideration determining their morality, so far he was indisputably in the right path: though to go far in it without wandering, there was needed a greater knowledge of the formation of character, and of the consequences of actions upon the agent's own frame of mind, than Bentham possessed. His want of power to estimate this class of consequences, together with his want of the degree of modest deference which, from those who have not competent experience of their own, is due to the experience of others on that part of the subject, greatly limit the value of his speculations on questions of practical ethics.

He is chargeable also with another error, which it would be improper to pass over, because nothing has tended more to place him in opposition to the common feelings of mankind, and to give to his philosophy that

cold, mechanical, and ungenial air which characterizes
the popular idea of a Benthamite. This error, or rather
one-sidedness, belongs to him not as a utilitarian, but
as a moralist by profession, and in common with
almost all professed moralists, whether religious or
philosophical: it is that of treating the *moral* view of
actions and characters, which is unquestionably the
first and most important mode of looking at them, as
if it were the sole one: whereas it is only one of three,
by all of which our sentiments towards the human
being may be, ought to be, and without entirely crush-
ing our own nature cannot but be, materially influenced. Every human action has three aspects: its
moral aspect, or that of its *right* and *wrong*; its *æsthetic*
aspect, or that of its *beauty*; its *sympathetic* aspect, or
that of its *loveableness*. The first addresses itself to our
reason and conscience; the second to our imagination;
the third to our human fellow-feeling. According to
the first, we approve or disapprove; according to the
second, we admire or despise; according to the third,
we love, pity, or dislike. The morality of an action
depends on its foreseeable consequences; its beauty,
and its loveableness, or the reverse, depend on the
qualities which it is evidence of. Thus, a lie is *wrong*,
because its effect is to mislead, and because it tends to
destroy the confidence of man in man; it is also *mean*,
because it is cowardly—because it proceeds from not
daring to face the consequences of telling the truth—
or at best is evidence of want of that *power* to compass
our ends by straightforward means, which is conceived
as properly belonging to every person not deficient in
energy or in understanding. The action of Brutus in
sentencing his sons was *right*, because it was executing
a law essential to the freedom of his country, against

93

persons of whose guilt there was no doubt: it was *admirable*, because it evinced a rare degree of patriotism, courage, and self-control; but there was nothing *loveable* in it; it affords either no presumption in regard to loveable qualities, or a presumption of their deficiency. If one of the sons had engaged in the conspiracy from affection for the other, his action would have been loveable, though neither moral nor admirable. It is not possible for any sophistry to confound these three modes of viewing an action; but it is very possible to adhere to one of them exclusively, and lose sight of the rest. Sentimentality consists in setting the last two of the three above the first; the error of moralists in general, and of Bentham, is to sink the two latter entirely. This is pre-eminently the case with Bentham: he both wrote and felt as if the moral standard ought not only to be paramount (which it ought), but to be alone; as if it ought to be the sole master of all our actions, and even of all our sentiments; as if either to admire or like, or despise or dislike a person for any action which neither does good nor harm, or which does not do a good or a harm proportioned to the sentiment entertained, were an injustice and a prejudice. He carried this so far, that there were certain phrases which, being expressive of what he considered to be this groundless liking or aversion, he could not bear to hear pronounced in his presence. Among these phrases were those of *good* and *bad taste*. He thought it an insolent piece of dogmatism in one person to praise or condemn another in a matter of taste: as if men's likings and dislikings, on things in themselves indifferent, were not full of the most important inferences as to every point of their character; as if a person's tastes did not show him to be wise or a fool, cultivated or ignorant, gentle or rough, sensitive or callous, generous or sordid, benevolent or selfish, conscientious or depraved.

Connected with the same topic are Bentham's peculiar opinions on poetry. Much more has been said than there is any foundation for, about his contempt for the pleasures of imagination, and for the fine arts. Music was throughout life his favourite amusement; painting, sculpture, and the other arts addressed to the eye, he was so far from holding in any contempt, that he occasionally recognises them as means employable for important social ends; though his ignorance of the deeper springs of human character prevented him (as it prevents most Englishmen) from suspecting how profoundly such things enter into the moral nature of man, and into the education both of the individual and of the race. But towards poetry in the narrower sense, that which employs the language of words, he entertained no favour. Words, he thought, were perverted from their proper office when they were employed in uttering anything but precise logical truth. He says, somewhere in his works, that, 'quantity of pleasure being equal, push-pin is as good as poetry:' but this is only a paradoxical way of stating what he would equally have said of the things which he most valued and admired. Another aphorism is attributed to him, which is much more characteristic of his view of this subject: 'All poetry is misrepresentation.' Poetry, he thought, consisted essentially in exaggeration for effect: in proclaiming some one view of a thing very emphatically, and suppressing all the limitations and qualifications. This trait of character seems to us a curious example of what Mr. Carlyle strikingly calls 'the completeness of limited men.' Here is a philosopher who is happy within his narrow boundary as no man of indefinite range ever was: who flatters himself that he is so completely emancipated from the essential law of poor human intellect, by which it can only see one thing at a time well, that he can even turn round upon the imperfection and lay a solemn interdict upon it. Did Bentham really suppose that it is in poetry only that propositions cannot be exactly true, cannot contain in themselves all the limitations and qualifications with which they require to be taken when applied to practice? We have seen how far his own prose propositions are from realizing this Utopia: and even the attempt to approach it would be incompatible not with poetry merely, but with oratory, and popular writing of every kind. Bentham's charge is true to the fullest extent; all writing which undertakes to make men feel truths as well as see them, does take up one point at a time, does seek to impress that, to drive that home, to make it sink into and colour the whole mind of the reader or hearer. It is justified in doing so, if the portion of truth which it thus enforces be that which is called for by the occasion. All writing addressed to the feelings has a natural tendency to exaggeration; but Bentham should have remembered that in this, as in many things, we must aim at too much, to be assured of doing enough.

From the same principle in Bentham came the intricate and involved style, which makes his later writings books for the student only, not the general reader. It was from his perpetually aiming at impracticable precision. Nearly all his earlier, and many parts of his later writings, are models, as we have already observed, of light, playful, and popular style: a Benthamiana might be made of passages worthy of Addison or Goldsmith.

But in his later years and more advanced studies, he fell into a Latin or German structure of sentence, foreign to the genius of the English language. He could not bear, for the sake of clearness and the reader's ease, to say, as ordinary men are content to do, a little more than the truth in one sentence, and correct it in the next. The whole of the qualifying remarks which he intended to make, he insisted upon imbedding as parentheses in the very middle of the sentence itself. And thus the sense being so long suspended, and attention being required to the accessory ideas before the principal idea had been properly seized, it became difficult, without some practice, to make out the train of thought. It is fortunate that so many of the most important parts of his writings are free from this defect. We regard it as a *reductio ad absurdum* of his objection to poetry. In trying to write in a manner against which the same objection should not lie, he could stop nowhere short of utter unreadableness, and after all attained no more accuracy than is compatible with opinions as imperfect and one-sided as those of any poet or sentimentalist breathing. Judge then in what state literature and philosophy would be, and what chance they would have of influencing the multitude, if his objection were allowed, and all styles of writing banished which would not stand his test.

We must here close this brief and imperfect view of Bentham and his doctrines; in which many parts of the subject have been entirely untouched, and no part done justice to, but which at least proceeds from an intimate familiarity with his writings, and is nearly the first attempt at an impartial estimate of his character as a philosopher, and of the result of his labours to the world.

After every abatement, and it has been seen whether we have made our abatements sparingly—there remains to Bentham an indisputable place among the great intellectual benefactors of mankind. His writings will long form an indispensable part of the education of the highest order of practical thinkers; and the collected edition of them ought to be in the hands of every one who would either understand his age, or take any beneficial part in the great business of it.[1]

---

[1] Since the first publication of this paper, Lord Brougham's brilliant series of characters has been published, including a sketch of Bentham. Lord Brougham's view of Bentham's characteristics agrees in the main points, so far as it goes, with the result of our more minute examination, but there is an imputation cast upon Bentham, of a jealous and splenetic disposition in private life, of which we feel called upon to give at once a contradiction and an explanation. It is indispensable to a correct estimate of any of Bentham's dealings with the world, to bear in mind that in everything except abstract speculation he was to the last, what we have called him, essentially a boy. He had the freshness, the simplicity, the confidingness, the liveliness and activity, all the delightful qualities of boyhood, and the weaknesses which are the reverse side of those qualities—the undue importance attached to trifles, the habitual mismeasurement of the practical bearing and value of things, the readiness to be either delighted or offended on inadequate cause. These were the real sources of what was unreasonable in some of his attacks on individuals, and in particular on Lord Brougham, on the subject of his Law Reforms; they were no more the effect of envy or malice, or any really unamiable quality, than the freaks of a pettish child, and are scarcely a fitter subject of censure or criticism.

an entire stranger to it: the other looked at it from
within, and endeavoured to see it with the eyes of a
believer in it; to discover by what apparent facts it
was at first suggested, and by what appearances it has
ever since been rendered continually credible—has
seemed, to a succession of persons, to be a faithful
interpretation of their experience. Bentham judged a
proposition true or false as it accorded or not with the
result of his own inquiries; and did not search very
curiously into what might be meant by the proposition, when it obviously did not mean what he thought
true. With Coleridge, on the contrary, the very fact
that any doctrine had been believed by thoughtful
men, and received by whole nations or generations of
mankind, was part of the problem to be solved, was
one of the phenomena to be accounted for. And as
Bentham's short and easy method of referring all to
the selfish interests of aristocracies, or priests, or lawyers, or some other species of impostors, could not
satisfy a man who saw so much farther into the complexities of the human intellect and feelings—he considered the long or extensive prevalence of any opinion
as a presumption that it was not altogether a fallacy;
that, to its first authors at least, it was the result of a
struggle to express in words something which had a
reality to them, though perhaps not to many of those
who have since received the doctrine by mere tradition. The long duration of a belief, he thought, is at
least proof of an adaptation in it to some portion or
other of the human mind; and if, on digging down to
the root, we do not find, as is generally the case, some
truth, we shall find some natural want or requirement
of human nature which the doctrine in question is
fitted to satisfy: among which wants the instincts of

selfishness and of credulity have a place, but by no means an exclusive one. From this difference in the points of view of the two philosophers, and from the too rigid adherence of each to his own, it was to be expected that Bentham should continually miss the truth which is in the traditional opinions, and Coleridge that which is out of them, and at variance with them. But it was also likely that each would find, or show the way to finding, much of what the other missed.

It is hardly possible to speak of Coleridge, and his position among his contemporaries, without reverting to Bentham: they are connected by two of the closest bonds of association—resemblance, and contrast. It would be difficult to find two persons of philosophic eminence more exactly the contrary of one another. Compare their modes of treatment of any subject, and you might fancy them inhabitants of different worlds. They seem to have scarcely a principle or a premise in common. Each of them sees scarcely anything but what the other does not see. Bentham would have regarded Coleridge with a peculiar measure of the good-humoured contempt with which he was accustomed to regard all modes of philosophizing different from his own. Coleridge would probably have made Bentham one of the exceptions to the enlarged and liberal appreciation which (to the credit of *his* mode of philosophizing) he extended to most thinkers of any eminence, from whom he differed. But contraries, as logicians say, are but *quæ in eodem genere maxime distant*, the things which are farthest from one another in the same kind. These two agreed in being the men who, in their age and country, did most to enforce, by precept and example, the necessity of a philosophy.

They agreed in making it their occupation to recall opinions to first principles; taking no proposition for granted without examining into the grounds of it, and ascertaining that it possessed the kind and degree of evidence suitable to its nature. They agreed in recognising that sound theory is the only foundation for sound practice, and that whoever despises theory, let him give himself what airs of wisdom he may, is self-convicted of being a quack. If a book were to be compiled containing all the best things ever said on the rule-of-thumb school of political craftsmanship, and on the insufficiency for practical purposes of what the mere practical man calls experience, it is difficult to say whether the collection would be more indebted to the writings of Bentham or of Coleridge. They agreed, too, in perceiving that the groundwork of all other philosophy must be laid in the philosophy of the mind. To lay this foundation deeply and strongly, and to raise a superstructure in accordance with it, were the objects to which their lives were devoted. They employed, indeed, for the most part, different materials; but as the materials of both were real observations, the genuine product of experience—the results will in the end be found not hostile, but supplementary, to one another. Of their methods of philosophizing, the same thing may be said: they were different, yet both were legitimate logical processes. In every respect the two men are each other's 'completing counterpart': the strong points of each correspond to the weak points of the other. Whoever could master the premises and combine the methods of both, would possess the entire English philosophy of his age. Coleridge used to say that every one is born either a Platonist or an Aristotelian: it may be similarly affirmed, that every Englishman of the present day is by implication either a Benthamite or a Coleridgian; holds views of human affairs which can only be proved true on the principles either of Bentham or of Coleridge. In one respect, indeed, the parallel fails. Bentham so improved and added to the system of philosophy he adopted, that for his successors he may almost be accounted its founder; while Coleridge, though he has left on the system he inculcated, such traces of himself as cannot fail to be left by any mind of original powers, was anticipated in all the essentials of his doctrine by the great Germans of the latter half of the last century, and was accompanied in it by the remarkable series of their French expositors and followers. Hence, although Coleridge is to Englishmen the type and the main source of that doctrine, he is the creator rather of the shape in which it has appeared among us, than of the doctrine itself.

The time is yet far distant when, in the estimation of Coleridge, and of his influence upon the intellect of our time, anything like unanimity can be looked for. As a poet, Coleridge has taken his place. The healthier taste, and more intelligent canons of poetic criticism, which he was himself mainly instrumental in diffusing, have at length assigned to him his proper rank, as one among the great, and (if we look to the powers shown rather than to the amount of actual achievement) among the greatest, names in our literature. But as a philosopher, the class of thinkers has scarcely yet arisen by whom he is to be judged. The limited philosophical public of this country is as yet too exclusively divided between those to whom Coleridge and the views which he promulgated or defended are everything, and those to whom they are nothing. A true thinker can only be justly estimated when his thoughts have worked their way into minds formed in a different school; have been wrought and moulded into consistency with all other true and relevant thoughts; when the noisy conflict of half-truths, angrily denying one another, has subsided, and ideas which seemed mutually incompatible, have been found only to require mutual limitations. This time has not yet come for Coleridge. The spirit of philosophy in England, like that of religion, is still rootedly sectarian. Conservative thinkers and Liberals, transcendentalists and admirers of Hobbes and Locke, regard each other as out of the pale of philosophical intercourse; look upon each other's speculations as vitiated by an original taint, which makes all study of them, except for purposes of attack, useless, if not mischievous. An error much the same as if Kepler had refused to profit by Ptolemy's or Tycho's observations, because those astronomers believed that the sun moved round the earth; or as if Priestley and Lavoisier, because they differed on the doctrine of phlogiston, had rejected each other's chemical experiments. It is even a still greater error than either of these. For, among the truths long recognised by Continental philosophers, but which very few Englishmen have yet arrived at, one is, the importance, in the present imperfect state of mental and social science, of antagonist modes of thought: which, it will one day be felt, are as necessary to one another in speculation, as mutually checking powers are in a political constitution. A clear insight, indeed, into this necessity is the only rational or enduring basis of philosophical tolerance; the only condition under which liberality in matters of opinion can be anything better than a polite synonym for indifference between one opinion and another.

All students of man and society who possess that first requisite for so difficult a study, a due sense of its difficulties, are aware that the besetting danger is not so much of embracing falsehood for truth, as of mistaking part of the truth for the whole. It might be plausibly maintained that in almost every one of the leading controversies, past or present, in social philosophy, both sides were in the right in what they affirmed, though wrong in what they denied; and that if either could have been made to take the other's views in addition to its own, little more would have been needed to make its doctrine correct. Take for instance the question how far mankind have gained by civilization. One observer is forcibly struck by the multiplication of physical comforts; the advancement and diffusion of knowledge; the decay of superstition; the facilities of mutual intercourse; the softening of manners; the decline of war and personal conflict; the progressive limitation of the tyranny of the strong over the weak; the great works accomplished throughout the globe by the co-operation of multitudes: and he becomes that very common character, the worshipper of 'our enlightened age.' Another fixes his attention, not upon the value of these advantages, but upon the high price which is paid for them; the relaxation of individual energy and courage; the loss of proud and self-relying independence; the slavery of so large a portion of mankind to artificial wants; their effeminate shrinking from even the shadow of pain; the dull unexciting monotony of their lives, and the passionless insipidity, and absence of any marked individuality, in their characters; the contrast between the narrow mechanical understanding, produced by a life spent in executing by fixed rules a fixed task, and the varied powers of the man of the woods, whose subsistence and safety depend at each instant upon his capacity of extemporarily adapting means to ends; the demoralizing effect of great inequalities in wealth and social rank; and the sufferings of the great mass of the people of civilized countries, whose wants are scarcely better provided for than those of the savage, while they are bound by a thousand fetters in lieu of the freedom and excitement which are his compensations. One who attends to these things, and to these exclusively, will be apt to infer that savage life is preferable to civilized; that the work of civilization should as far as possible be undone; and from the premises of Rousseau, he will not improbably be led to the practical conclusions of Rousseau's disciple, Robespierre. No two thinkers can be more entirely at variance than the two we have supposed—the worshippers of Civilization and of Independence, of the present and of the remote past. Yet all that is positive in the opinions of either of them is true; and we see how easy it would be to choose one's path, if either half of the truth were the whole of it, and how great may be the difficulty of framing, as it is necessary to do, a set of practical maxims which combine both.

So again, one person sees in a very strong light the need which the great mass of mankind have of being ruled over by a degree of intelligence and virtue superior to their own. He is deeply impressed with the mischief done to the uneducated and uncultivated by weaning them of all habits of reverence, appealing to them as a competent tribunal to decide the most intricate questions, and making them think themselves capable, not only of being a light to themselves, but of giving the law to their superiors in culture. He sees, further, that cultivation, to be carried beyond a certain point, requires leisure; that leisure is the natural attribute of a hereditary aristocracy; that such a body has all the means of acquiring intellectual and moral superiority; and he needs be at no loss to endow them with abundant motives to it. An aristocracy indeed, being human, are, as he cannot but see, not exempt, any more than their inferiors, from the common need of being controlled and enlightened by a still greater wisdom and goodness than their own. For this, however, his reliance is upon reverence for a Higher above them, sedulously inculcated and fostered by the course of their education. We thus see brought together all the elements of a conscientious zealot for an aristocratic government, supporting and supported by an established Christian church. There is truth, and important truth, in this thinker's premises. But there is a thinker of a very different description, in whose premises there is an equal portion of truth. This is he who says, that an average man, even an average member of an aristocracy, if he can postpone the interests of other people to his own calculations or instincts of self-interest, will do so; that all governments in all ages have done so, as far as they were permitted, and generally to a ruinous extent; and that the only possible remedy is a pure democracy, in which the people are their own governors, and can have no selfish interest in oppressing themselves.

Thus it is in regard to every important partial truth; there are always two conflicting modes of thought, one tending to give to that truth too large, the other to give it too small, a place: and the history of opinion is generally an oscillation between these extremes. From the imperfection of the human faculties, it seldom happens that, even in the minds of eminent thinkers, each partial view of their subject passes for its worth, and none for more than its worth. But even if this just balance exist in the mind of the wiser teacher, it will not exist in his disciples, less in the general mind. He cannot prevent that which is new in his doctrine, and on which, being new, he is forced to insist the most strongly, from making a disproportionate impression. The impetus necessary to overcome the obstacles which resist all novelties of opinion, seldom fails to carry the public mind almost as far on the contrary side of the perpendicular. Thus every excess in either direction determines a corresponding reaction; improvement consisting only in this, that the oscillation, each time, departs rather less widely from the centre, and an ever-increasing tendency is manifested to settle finally in it.

Now the Germano-Coleridgian doctrine is, in our view of the matter, the result of such a reaction. It expresses the revolt of the human mind against the philosophy of the eighteenth century. It is ontological, because that was experimental; conservative, because that was innovative; religious, because so much of that was infidel; concrete and historical, because that was abstract and metaphysical; poetical, because that was matter-of-fact and prosaic. In every respect it flies off in the contrary direction to its predecessor; yet faithful to the general law of improvement last noticed, it is less extreme in its opposition, it denies less of what is true in the doctrine it wars against, than had been the case in any previous philosophic reaction; and in particular, far less than when the philosophy of the eighteenth century triumphed, and so memorably abused its victory, over that which preceded it.

We may begin our consideration of the two systems either at one extreme or the other; with their highest philosophical generalizations, or with their practical conclusions. The former seems preferable, because it is in their highest generalities that the difference between the two systems is most familiarly known.

Every consistent scheme of philosophy requires as its starting-point, a theory respecting the sources of human knowledge, and the objects which the human faculties are capable of taking cognizance of. The prevailing theory in the eighteenth century, on this most comprehensive of questions, was that proclaimed by Locke, and commonly attributed to Aristotle—that all knowledge consists of generalizations from experience. Of nature, or anything whatever external to ourselves, we know, according to this theory, nothing, except the facts which present themselves to our senses, and such other facts as may, by analogy, be inferred from these. There is no knowledge *à priori*; no truths cognizable by the mind's inward light, and grounded on intuitive evidence. Sensation, and the mind's consciousness of its own acts, are not only the exclusive sources, but the sole materials of our knowledge. From this doctrine, Coleridge, with the German philosophers since Kant (not to go farther back) and most of the English since Reid, strongly dissents. He claims for the human mind a capacity, within certain limits, of perceiving the nature and properties of 'Things in themselves.' He distinguishes in the human intellect two faculties, which, in the technical language common to him with the Germans, he calls Understanding and Reason. The former faculty judges of phenomena, or the appearances of things, and forms generalizations from these: to the latter it belongs, by direct intuition, to perceive things, and recognise truths, not cognizable by our senses. These perceptions are not indeed innate, nor could ever have been awakened in us without experience; but they are not copies of it: experience is not their prototype, it is only the occasion by which they are irresistibly suggested. The appearances in nature excite in us, by an inherent law, ideas of those invisible things which are the causes of the visible appearances, and on whose laws those appearances depend: and we then perceive that these things must have pre-existed to render the appearances possible; just as (to use a frequent illustration of Coleridge's) we see, before we know that we have eyes; but when once this is known to us, we perceive that eyes must have pre-existed to enable us to see. Among the truths which are thus known *à priori*, by occasion of experience, but not themselves the subjects of experience, Coleridge includes the fundamental doctrines of religion and morals, the principles of mathematics, and the ultimate laws even of physical nature; which he contends cannot be proved by experience, though they must necessarily be consistent with it, and would, if we knew them perfectly, enable us to account for all observed facts, and to predict all those which are as yet unobserved.

It is not necessary to remind any one who concerns himself with such subjects, that between the partisans of these two opposite doctrines there reigns a *bellum internecinum*. Neither side is sparing in the imputation of intellectual and moral obliquity to the perceptions, and of pernicious consequences to the creed, of its antagonists. Sensualism is the common term of abuse for the one philosophy, mysticism for the other. The one doctrine is accused of making men beasts, the other lunatics. It is the unaffected belief of numbers on one side of the controversy, that their adversaries are actuated by a desire to break loose from moral and religious obligation; and of numbers on the other that their opponents are either men fit for Bedlam, or who cunningly pander to the interests of hierarchies and aristocracies, by manufacturing superfine new arguments in favour of old prejudices. It is almost needless to say that those who are freest with these mutual accusations, are seldom those who are most at home in the real intricacies of the question, or who are best acquainted with the argumentative strength of the opposite side, or even of their own. But without going to these extreme lengths, even sober men on both sides take no charitable view of the tendencies of each other's opinions.

It is affirmed that the doctrine of Locke and his followers, that all knowledge is experience generalized, leads by strict logical consequence to atheism: that Hume and other sceptics were right when they contended that it is impossible to prove a God on grounds of experience; and Coleridge (like Kant) maintains positively, that the ordinary argument for a Deity, from marks of design in the universe, or, in other words, from the resemblance of the order in nature to the effects of human skill and contrivance, is not tenable. It is further said that the same doctrine annihilates moral obligation; reducing morality either to the blind impulses of animal sensibility, or to a calculation of prudential consequences, both equally fatal to its essence. Even science, it is affirmed, loses the character

111

of science in this view of it, and becomes empiricism; a mere enumeration and arrangement of facts, not explaining nor accounting for them: since a fact is only then accounted for, when we are made to see in it the manifestation of laws, which, as soon as they are perceived at all, are perceived to be *necessary*. These are the charges brought by the transcendental philosophers against the school of Locke, Hartley, and Bentham. They in their turn allege that the transcendentalists make imagination, and not observation, the criterion of truth; that they lay down principles under which a man may enthrone his wildest dreams in the chair of philosophy, and impose them on mankind as intuitions of the pure reason: which has, in fact, been done in all ages, by all manner of mystical enthusiasts. And even if, with gross inconsistency, the private revelations of any individual Behmen or Swedenborg be disowned, or, in other words, outvoted (the only means of discrimination which, it is contended, the theory admits of), this is still only substituting, as the test of truth, the dreams of the majority for the dreams of each individual. Whoever form a strong enough party, may at any time set up the immediate perceptions of *their* reason, that is to say, any reigning prejudice, as a truth independent of experience; a truth not only requiring no proof, but to be believed in opposition to all that appears proof to the mere understanding; nay, the more to be believed, because it cannot be put into words and into the logical form of a proposition without a contradiction in terms: for no less authority than this is claimed by some transcendentalists for their *à priori* truths. And thus a ready mode is provided, by which whoever is on the strongest side may dogmatize at his ease, and instead of proving his propositions, may rail at all who deny them, as bereft of 'the vision and the faculty divine,' or blinded to its plainest revelations by a corrupt heart.

This is a very temperate statement of what is charged by these two classes of thinkers against each other. How much of either representation is correct, cannot conveniently be discussed in this place. In truth, a system of consequences from an opinion, drawn by an adversary, is seldom of much worth. Disputants are rarely sufficiently masters of each other's doctrines, to be good judges what is fairly deducible from them, or how a consequence which seems to flow from one part of the theory may or may not be defeated by another part. To combine the different parts of a doctrine with one another, and with all admitted truths, is not indeed a small trouble, nor one which a person is often inclined to take for other people's opinions. Enough if each does it for his own, which he has a greater interest in, and is more disposed to be just to. Were we to search among men's recorded thoughts for the choicest manifestations of human imbecility and prejudice, our specimens would be mostly taken from their opinions of the opinions of one another. Imputations of horrid consequences ought not to bias the judgment of any person capable of independent thought. Coleridge himself says (in the 25th Aphorism of his 'Aids to Reflection'), 'He who begins by loving Christianity better than truth, will proceed by loving his own sect or church better than Christianity, and end in loving himself better than all.'

As to the fundamental difference of opinion respecting the sources of our knowledge (apart from the corollaries which either party may have drawn from its own principle, or imputed to its opponent's), the question lies far too deep in the recesses of psychology for us to discuss it here. The lists having been open ever since the dawn of philosophy, it is not wonderful that the two parties should have been forced to put on their strongest armour, both of attack and of defence. The question would not so long have remained a question, if the more obvious arguments on either side had been unanswerable. Each party has been able to urge in its own favour numerous and striking facts, to reconcile which with the opposite theory has required all the metaphysical resources which that theory could command. It will not be wondered at, then, that we here content ourselves with a bare statement of our opinion. It is, that the truth, on this much-debated question, lies with the school of Locke and of Bentham. The nature and laws of Things in themselves, or of the hidden causes of the phenomena which are the objects of experience, appear to us radically inaccessible to the human faculties. We see no ground for believing that anything can be the object of our knowledge except our experience, and what can be inferred from our experience by the analogies of experience itself; nor that there is any idea, feeling, or power in the human mind, which, in order to account for it, requires that its origin should be referred to any other source. We are therefore at issue with Coleridge on the central idea of his philosophy; and we find no need of, and no use for, the peculiar technical terminology which he and his masters the Germans have introduced into philosophy, for the double purpose of giving logical precision to doctrines which we do not admit, and of marking a relation between those abstract doctrines and many concrete experimental truths, which this language, in our judgment, serves not to elucidate, but

to disguise and obscure. Indeed, but for these peculiarities of language, it would be difficult to understand
how the reproach of mysticism (by which nothing is
meant in common parlance but unintelligibleness) has
been fixed upon Coleridge and the Germans in the
minds of many, to whom doctrines substantially the
same, when taught in a manner more superficial and
less fenced round against objections, by Reid and
Dugald Stewart, have appeared the plain dictates of
'common sense,' successfully asserted against the
subtleties of metaphysics.

Yet, though we think the doctrines of Coleridge and
the Germans, in the pure science of mind, erroneous,
and have no taste for their peculiar terminology, we
are far from thinking that even in respect of this, the
least valuable part of their intellectual exertions, those
philosophers have lived in vain. The doctrines of the
school of Locke stood in need of an entire renovation:
to borrow a physiological illustration from Coleridge,
they required, like certain secretions of the human
body, to be reabsorbed into the system and secreted
afresh. In what form did that philosophy generally
prevail throughout Europe? In that of the shallowest
set of doctrines which perhaps were ever passed off
upon a cultivated age as a complete psychological
system—the ideology of Condillac and his school; a
system which affected to resolve all the phenomena of
the human mind into sensation, by a process which
essentially consisted in merely *calling* all states of
mind, however heterogeneous, by that name; a philosophy now acknowledged to consist solely of a set of
verbal generalizations, explaining nothing, distinguish-
ing nothing, leading to nothing. That men should begin
by sweeping this away, was the first sign that the age

of real psychology was about to commence. In England the case, though different, was scarcely better. The philosophy of Locke, as a popular doctrine, had remained nearly as it stood in his own book; which, as its title implies, did not pretend to give an account of any but the intellectual part of our nature; which, even within that limited sphere, was but the commencement of a system, and though its errors and defects as such have been exaggerated beyond all just bounds, it did expose many vulnerable points to the searching criticism of the new school. The least imperfect part of it, the purely logical part, had almost dropped out of sight. With respect to those of Locke's doctrines which are properly metaphysical; however the sceptical part of them may have been followed up by others, and carried beyond the point at which he stopped; the only one of his successors who attempted, and achieved, any considerable improvement and extension of the analytical part, and thereby added anything to the explanation of the human mind on Locke's principles, was Hartley. But Hartley's doctrines, so far as they are true, were so much in advance of the age, and the way had been so little prepared for them by the general tone of thinking which yet prevailed, even under the influence of Locke's writings, that the philosophic world did not deem them worthy of being attended to. Reid and Stewart were allowed to run them down uncontradicted: Brown, though a man of a kindred genius, had evidently never read them; and but for the accident of their being taken up by Priestley, who transmitted them as a kind of heirloom to his Unitarian followers, the name of Hartley might have perished, or survived only as that of a visionary physician, the author of an exploded physiological hypothesis. It perhaps required all the violence of the assaults made by Reid and the German school upon Locke's system, to recall men's minds to Hartley's principles, as alone adequate to the solution, upon that system, of the peculiar difficulties which those assailants pressed upon men's attention as altogether insoluble by it. We may here notice that Coleridge, before he adopted his later philosophical views, was an enthusiastic Hartleian; so that his abandonment of the philosophy of Locke cannot be imputed to unacquaintance with the highest form of that philosophy which had yet appeared. That he should pass through that highest form without stopping at it, is itself a strong presumption that there were more difficulties in the question than Hartley had solved. That anything has since been done to solve them we probably owe to the revolution in opinion, of which Coleridge was one of the organs; and even in abstract metaphysics, his writings, and those of his school of thinkers, are the richest mine from whence the opposite school can draw the materials for what has yet to be done to perfect their own theory.

If we now pass from the purely abstract to the concrete and practical doctrines of the two schools, we shall see still more clearly the necessity of the reaction, and the great service rendered to philosophy by its authors. This will be best manifested by a survey of the state of practical philosophy in Europe, as Coleridge and his compeers found it, towards the close of the last century.

The state of opinion in the latter half of the eighteenth century was by no means the same on the Continent of Europe and in our own island; and the difference was still greater in appearance than it was in reality. In the more advanced nations of the

Continent, the prevailing philosophy had done its work completely: it had spread itself over every department of human knowledge; it had taken possession of the whole Continental mind: and scarcely one educated person was left who retained any allegiance to the opinions or the institutions of ancient times. In England, the native country of compromise, things had stopped far short of this; the philosophical movement had been brought to a halt in an early stage, and a peace had been patched up by concessions on both sides, between the philosophy of the time and its traditional institutions and creeds. Hence the aberrations of the age were generally, on the Continent, at that period, the extravagances of new opinions; in England, the corruptions of old ones.

To insist upon the deficiencies of the Continental philosophy of the last century, or, as it is commonly termed, the French philosophy, is almost superfluous. That philosophy is indeed as unpopular in this country as its bitterest enemy could desire. If its faults were as well understood as they are much railed at, criticism might be considered to have finished its work. But that this is not yet the case, the nature of the imputations currently made upon the French philosophers, sufficiently proves; many of these being as inconsistent with a just philosophic comprehension of their system of opinions, as with charity towards the men themselves. It is not true, for example, that any of them denied moral obligation, or sought to weaken its force. So far were they from meriting this accusation, that they could not even tolerate the writers who, like Helvetius, ascribed a selfish origin to the feelings of morality, resolving them into a sense of interest. Those writers were as much cried down among the

118

philosophes themselves, and what was true and good in them (and there is much that is so) met with as little appreciation, then as now. The error of the philosophers was rather that they trusted too much to those feelings; believed them to be more deeply rooted in human nature than they are; to be not so dependent, as in fact they are, upon collateral influences. They thought them the natural and spontaneous growth of the human heart; so firmly fixed in it, that they would subsist unimpaired, nay invigorated, when the whole system of opinions and observances with which they were habitually intertwined was violently torn away.

To tear away was, indeed, all that these philosophers, for the most part, aimed at: they had no conception that anything else was needful. At their millennium, superstition, priestcraft, error and prejudice of every kind, were to be annihilated; some of them gradually added that despotism and hereditary privileges must share the same fate; and, this accomplished, they never for a moment suspected that all the virtues and graces of humanity could fail to flourish, or that when the noxious weeds were once rooted out, the soil would stand in any need of tillage.

In this they committed the very common error, of mistaking the state of things with which they had always been familiar, for the universal and natural condition of mankind. They were accustomed to see the human race agglomerated in large nations, all (except here and there a madman or a malefactor) yielding obedience more or less strict to a set of laws prescribed by a few of their own number, and to a set of moral rules prescribed by each other's opinion; renouncing the exercise of individual will and judgment, except within the limits imposed by these laws and

rules; and acquiescing in the sacrifice of their individual wishes when the point was decided against them
by lawful authority; or persevering only in hopes of
altering the opinion of the ruling powers. Finding
matters to be so generally in this condition, the philosophers apparently concluded that they could not
possibly be in any other; and were ignorant, by what
a host of civilizing and restraining influences a state
of things so repugnant to man's self-will and love
of independence has been brought about, and how
imperatively it demands the continuance of those
influences as the condition of its own existence. The
very first element of the social union, obedience to a
government of some sort, has not been found so easy
a thing to establish in the world. Among a timid and
spiritless race, like the inhabitants of the vast plains of
tropical countries, passive obedience may be of natural
growth; though even there we doubt whether it has
ever been found among any people with whom fatalism,
or in other words, submission to the pressure of circumstances as the decree of God, did not prevail as
a religious doctrine. But the difficulty of inducing a
brave and warlike race to submit their individual
arbitrium to any common umpire, has always been
felt to be so great, that nothing short of supernatural
power has been deemed adequate to overcome it; and
such tribes have always assigned to the first institution
of civil society a divine origin. So differently did those
judge who knew savage man by actual experience,
from those who had no acquaintance with him except
in the civilized state. In modern Europe itself, after the
fall of the Roman empire, to subdue the feudal anarchy
and bring the whole people of any European nation
into subjection to government (although Christianity

in the most concentrated form of its influence was co-operating in the work) required thrice as many centuries as have elapsed since that time.

Now if these philosophers had known human nature under any other type than that of their own age, and of the particular classes of society among whom they lived, it would have occurred to them, that wherever this habitual submission to law and government has been firmly and durably established, and yet the vigour and manliness of character which resisted its establishment have been in any degree preserved, certain requisites have existed, certain conditions have been fulfilled, of which the following may be regarded as the principal.

First: There has existed, for all who were accounted citizens,—for all who were not slaves, kept down by brute force,—a system of *education*, beginning with infancy and continued through life, of which, whatever else it might include, one main and incessant ingredient was *restraining discipline*. To train the human being in the habit, and thence the power, of subordinating his personal impulses and aims, to what were considered the ends of society; of adhering, against all temptation, to the course of conduct which those ends prescribed; of controlling in himself all the feelings which were liable to militate against those ends, and encouraging all such as tended towards them; this was the purpose, to which every outward motive that the authority directing the system could command, and every inward power or principle which its knowledge of human nature enabled it to evoke, were endeavoured to be rendered instrumental. The entire civil and military policy of the ancient commonwealths was such a system of training: in modern nations its place has been attempted to be supplied principally by religious teaching. And whenever and in proportion as the strictness of the restraining discipline was relaxed, the natural tendency of mankind to anarchy reasserted itself; the State became disorganized from within; mutual conflict for selfish ends, neutralized the energies which were required to keep up the contest against natural causes of evil; and the nation, after a longer or briefer interval of progressive decline, became either the slave of a despotism, or the prey of a foreign invader.

The second condition of permanent political society has been found to be, the existence, in some form or other, of the feeling of allegiance, or loyalty. This feeling may vary in its objects, and is not confined to any particular form of government; but whether in a democracy or in a monarchy, its essence is always the same; viz. that there be in the constitution of the State *something* which is settled, something permanent, and not to be called in question; something which, by general agreement, has a right to be where it is, and to be secure against disturbance, whatever else may change. This feeling may attach itself, as among the Jews (and indeed in most of the commonwealths of antiquity), to a common God or gods, the protectors and guardians of their State. Or it may attach itself to certain persons, who are deemed to be, whether by divine appointment, by long prescription, or by the general recognition of their superior capacity and worthiness, the rightful guides and guardians of the rest. Or it may attach itself to laws; to ancient liberties, or ordinances. Or finally (and this is the only shape in which the feeling is likely to exist hereafter) it may attach itself to the principles of individual freedom and political and social equality, as realized in institutions

which as yet exist nowhere, or exist only in a rudi-
mentary state. But in all political societies which have
had a durable existence, there has been some fixed
point; something which men agreed in holding sacred;
which, wherever freedom of discussion was a recognised principle, it was of course lawful to contest in
theory, but which no one could either fear or hope to
see shaken in practice; which, in short (except perhaps
during some temporary crisis), was in the common
estimation placed beyond discussion. And the necessity
of this may easily be made evident. A State never is,
nor, until mankind are vastly improved, can hope to
be, for any long time exempt from internal dissension;
for there neither is, nor has ever been, any state of
society in which collisions did not occur between the
immediate interests and passions of powerful sections
of the people. What, then, enables society to weather
these storms, and pass through turbulent times without any permanent weakening of the securities for
peaceable existence? Precisely this—that however important the interests about which men fall out, the
conflict did not affect the fundamental principles of the
system of social union which happened to exist; nor
threaten large portions of the community with the
subversion of that on which they had built their calculations, and with which their hopes and aims had
become identified. But when the questioning of these
fundamental principles is (not the occasional disease,
or salutary medicine, but) the habitual condition of
the body politic, and when all the violent animosities
are called forth, which spring naturally from such a
situation, the State is virtually in a position of civil
war; and can never long remain free from it in act and
fact.

The third essential condition of stability in political society, is a strong and active principle of cohesion among the members of the same community or state. We need scarcely say that we do not mean nationality, in the vulgar sense of the term; a senseless antipathy to foreigners; an indifference to the general welfare of the human race, or an unjust preference of the supposed interests of our own country; a cherishing of bad peculiarities because they are national; or a refusal to adopt what has been found good by other countries. We mean a principle of sympathy, not of hostility; of union, not of separation. We mean a feeling of common interest among those who live under the same government, and are contained within the same natural or historical boundaries. We mean, that one part of the community do not consider themselves as foreigners with regard to another part; that they set a value on their connexion; feel that they are one people, that their lot is cast together, that evil to any of their fellow-countrymen is evil to themselves; and do not desire selfishly to free themselves from their share of any common inconvenience by severing the connexion. How strong this feeling was in those ancient commonwealths which attained any durable greatness, every one knows. How happily Rome, in spite of all her tyranny, succeeded in establishing the feeling of a common country among the provinces of her vast and divided empire, will appear when any one who has given due attention to the subject shall take the trouble to point it out.[1] In modern times the coun-

---

[1] We are glad to quote a striking passage from Coleridge on this very subject. He is speaking of the misdeeds of England in Ireland; towards which misdeeds this Tory, as he is called (for the Tories, who neglected him in his lifetime, show no little eagerness to give themselves the credit of his name after his death), entertained feelings

tries which have had that feeling in the strongest degree have been the most powerful countries; England, France, and, in proportion to their territory scarcely surpassed by those which are excited by the masterly exposure for which we have recently been indebted to M. de Beaumont.

'Let us discharge,' he says, 'what may well be deemed a debt of justice from every well-educated Englishman to his Roman Catholic fellow-subjects of the Sister Island. At least, let us ourselves understand the true cause of the evil as it now exists. To what and to whom is the present state of Ireland mainly to be attributed? This should be the question: and to this I answer aloud, that it is mainly attributable to those who, during a period of little less than a whole century, used as a substitute what Providence had given into their hand as an opportunity; who chose to consider as superseding the most sacred duty, a code of law, which could be excused only on the plea that it enabled them to perform it. To the sloth and improvidence, the weakness and wickedness, of the gentry, clergy, and governors of Ireland, who persevered in preferring intrigue, violence, and selfish expatriation to a system of preventive and remedial measures, the efficacy of which had been warranted for them alike by the whole provincial history of ancient Rome, *cui pacare subactos summa erat sapientia*, and by the happy results of the few exceptions to the contrary scheme unhappily pursued by their and our ancestors.

'I can imagine no work of genius that would more appropriately decorate the dome or wall of a Senate-house, than an abstract of Irish history from the landing of Strongbow to the battle of the Boyne, or to a yet later period, embodied in intelligible emblems— an allegorical history-piece designed in the spirit of a Rubens or a Buonarotti, and with the wild lights, portentous shades, and saturated colours of a Rembrandt, Caravaggio, and Spagnoletti. To complete the great moral and political lesson by the historic contrast, nothing more would be required than by some equally effective means to possess the mind of the spectator with the state and condition of ancient Spain, at less than half a century from the final conclusion of an obstinate and almost unremitting conflict of two hundred years by Agrippa's subjugation of the Cantabrians, *omnibus Hispaniæ populis devictis et pacatis*. At the breaking up of the Empire the West Goths conquered the country, and made division of the lands. Then came eight centuries of Moorish domination. Yet so deeply had Roman wisdom impressed the fairest characters of the Roman mind, that at this very hour, if we except a comparatively insignificant portion of Arabic derivatives, the natives throughout the whole Peninsula speak a language less differing from the *Romana rustica*, or provincial Latin of the times of Lucan and Seneca, than any two of its dialects from each other. The time approaches, I trust, when our political economists may study the science of the provincial policy of the ancients in detail, under the auspices of hope, for immediate and practical purposes.'—*Church and State*, p. 161.

and resources, Holland and Switzerland; while England in her connexion with Ireland, is one of the most signal examples of the consequences of its absence. Every Italian knows why Italy is under a foreign yoke; every German knows what maintains despotism in the Austrian empire; the evils of Spain flow as much from the absence of nationality among the Spaniards themselves, as from the presence of it in their relations with foreigners; while the completest illustration of all is afforded by the republics of South America, where the parts of one and the same state adhere so slightly together, that no sooner does any province think itself aggrieved by the general government, than it proclaims itself a separate nation.

These essential requisites of civil society the French philosophers of the eighteenth century unfortunately overlooked. They found, indeed, all three—at least the first and second, and most of what nourishes and invigorates the third—already undermined by the vices of the institutions, and of the men, that were set up as the guardians and bulwarks of them. If innovators, in their theories, disregarded the elementary principles of the social union, Conservatives, in their practice, had set the first example. The existing order of things had ceased to realize those first principles: from the force of circumstances, and from the short-sighted selfishness of its administrators, it had ceased to possess the essential conditions of permanent society, and was therefore tottering to its fall. But the philosophers did not see this. Bad as the existing system was in the days of its decrepitude, according to them it was still worse when it actually did what it now only pretended to do. Instead of feeling that the effect of a bad social order in sapping the necessary foundations union, once lost, can ever be, or should be attempted to be, revived in connexion with the same institutions or the same doctrines as before. When society requires to be rebuilt, there is no use in attempting to rebuild it on the old plan. By the union of the enlarged views and analytic powers of speculative men with the observation and contriving sagacity of men of practice, better institutions and better doctrines must be elaborated; and until this is done we cannot hope for much improvement in our present condition. The effort to do it in the eighteenth century would have been premature, as the attempts of the Economistes (who, of all persons then living, came nearest to it, and who were the first to form clearly the idea of a Social Science), sufficiently testify. The time was not ripe for doing effectually any other work than that of destruction. But the work of the day should have been so performed as not to impede that of the morrow. No one can calculate what struggles, which the cause of improvement has yet to undergo, might have been spared if the philosophers of the eighteenth century had done anything like justice to the Past. Their mistake was, that they did not acknowledge the historical value of much which had ceased to be useful, nor saw that institutions and creeds, now effete, had rendered essential services to civilization, and still filled a place in the human mind, and in the arrangements of society, which could not without great peril be left vacant. Their mistake was, that they did not recognise in many of the errors which they assailed, corruptions of important truths, and in many of the institutions most cankered with abuse, necessary elements of civilized society, though in a form and vesture no longer suited to the age; and hence they involved, as far as in them lay, many great truths in a common discredit with the errors which had grown up around them. They threw away the shell without preserving the kernel; and attempting to new-model society without the binding forces which hold society together, met with such success as might have been anticipated.

Now we claim, in behalf of the philosophers of the reactionary school—of the school to which Coleridge belongs—that exactly what we blame the philosophers of the eighteenth century for not doing, they have done.

Every reaction in opinion, of course brings into view that portion of the truth which was overlooked before. It was natural that a philosophy which anathematized all that had been going on in Europe from Constantine to Luther, or even to Voltaire, should be succeeded by another, at once a severe critic of the new tendencies of society, and an impassioned vindicator of what was good in the past. This is the easy merit of all Tory and Royalist writers. But the peculiarity of the Germano-Coleridgian school is, that they saw beyond the immediate controversy, to the fundamental principles involved in all such controversies. They were the first (except a solitary thinker here and there) who inquired with any comprehensiveness or depth, into the inductive laws of the existence and growth of human society. They were the first to bring prominently forward the three requisites which we have enumerated, as essential principles of all permanent forms of social existence; as principles, we say, and not as mere accidental advantages inherent in the particular polity or religion which the writer happened to patronize. They were the first who pursued, philosophically and in the spirit of Baconian investigation, not only this inquiry, but others ulterior and collateral to it. They thus produced, not a piece of party advocacy, but a philosophy of society, in the only form in which it is yet possible, that of a philosophy of history; not a defence of particular ethical or religious doctrines, but a contribution, the largest made by any class of thinkers, towards the philosophy of human culture.

The brilliant light which has been thrown upon history during the last half century, has proceeded almost wholly from this school. The disrespect in which history was held by the *philosophes* is notorious; one of the soberest of them, D'Alembert we believe, was the author of the wish that all record whatever of past events could be blotted out. And indeed the ordinary mode of writing history, and the ordinary mode of drawing lessons from it, were almost sufficient to excuse this contempt. But the *philosophes* saw, as usual, what was not true, not what was. It is no wonder that they who looked on the greater part of what had been handed down from the past, as sheer hindrances to man's attaining a well-being which would otherwise be of easy attainment, should content themselves with a very superficial study of history. But the case was otherwise with those who regarded the maintenance of society at all, and especially its maintenance in a state of progressive advancement, as a very difficult task actually achieved, in however imperfect a manner, for a number of centuries, against the strongest obstacles. It was natural that they should feel a deep interest in ascertaining how this had been effected; and should be led to inquire, both what were the requisites of the permanent existence of see in the character of the national education existing in any political society, at once the principal cause of its permanence as a society, and the chief source of its progressiveness: the former by the extent to which that education operated as a system of restraining discipline; the latter by the degree in which it called forth and invigorated the active faculties. Besides, not to have looked upon the culture of the inward man as the problem of problems, would have been incompatible with the belief which many of these philosophers entertained in Christianity, and the recognition by all of them of its historical value, and the prime part which it has acted in the progress of mankind. But here, too, let us not fail to observe, they rose to principles, and did not stick in the particular case. The culture of the human being had been carried to no ordinary height, and human nature had exhibited many of its noblest manifestations, not in Christian countries only, but in the ancient world, in Athens, Sparta, Rome; nay, even barbarians, as the Germans, or still more unmitigated savages, the wild Indians, and again the Chinese, the Egyptians, the Arabs, all had their own education, their own culture; a culture which, whatever might be its tendency upon the whole, had been successful in some respect or other. Every form of polity, every condition of society, whatever else it had done, had formed its type of national character. What that type was, and how it had been made what it was, were questions which the metaphysician might overlook, the historical philosopher could not. Accordingly, the views respecting the various elements of human culture and the causes influencing the formation of national character, which pervade the writings of the Germano-Coleridgian school, throw into the shade everything

which had been effected before, or which has been
attempted simultaneously by any other school. Such
views are, more than anything else, the characteristic
feature of the Goethian period of German literature;
and are richly diffused through the historical and
critical writings of the new French school, as well as
of Coleridge and his followers.

In this long, though most compressed, dissertation
on the Continental philosophy preceding the reaction,
and on the nature of the reaction, so far as directed
against that philosophy, we have unavoidably been led
to speak rather of the movement itself, than of Coleridge's particular share in it; which, from his posteri-
ority in date, was necessarily a subordinate one. And it
would be useless, even did our limits permit, to bring
together from the scattered writings of a man who produced no systematic work, any of the fragments which
he may have contributed to an edifice still incomplete,
and even the general character of which, we can have
rendered very imperfectly intelligible to those who are
not acquainted with the theory itself. Our object is to
invite to the study of the original sources, not to supply
the place of such a study. What was peculiar to Coleridge will be better manifested, when we now proceed
to review the state of popular philosophy immediately
preceding him in our own island; which was different,
in some material respects, from the contemporaneous
Continental philosophy.

In England, the philosophical speculations of the
age had not, except in a few highly metaphysical minds
(whose example rather served to deter than to invite
others), taken so audacious a flight, nor achieved anything like so complete a victory over the counteracting

influences, as on the Continent. There is in the English mind, both in speculation and in practice, a highly salutary shrinking from all extremes. But as this shrinking is rather an instinct of caution than a result of insight, it is too ready to satisfy itself with any medium, merely because it is a medium, and to acquiesce in a union of the disadvantages of both extremes instead of their advantages. The circumstances of the age, too, were unfavourable to decided opinions. The repose which followed the great struggles of the Reformation and the Commonwealth; the final victory over Popery and Puritanism, Jacobitism and Republicanism, and the lulling of the controversies which kept speculation and spiritual consciousness alive; the lethargy which came upon all governors and teachers, after their position in society became fixed; and the growing absorption of all classes in material interests—caused a state of mind to diffuse itself, with less of deep inward workings, and less capable of interpreting those it had, than had existed for centuries. The age seemed smitten with an incapacity of producing deep or strong feeling, such as at least could ally itself with meditative habits. There were few poets, and none of a high order; and philosophy fell mostly into the hands of men of a dry prosaic nature, who had not enough of the materials of human feeling in them to be able to imagine any of its more complex and mysterious manifestations; all of which they either left out of their theories, or introduced them with such explanations as no one who had experienced the feelings could receive as adequate. An age like this, an age without earnestness, was the natural era of compromises and half-convictions.

To make out a case for the feudal and ecclesiastical

institutions of modern Europe was by no means impossible: they had a meaning, had existed for honest ends, and an honest theory of them might be made. But the administration of those institutions had long ceased to accord with any honest theory. It was impossible to justify them in principle, except on grounds which condemned them in practice; and grounds of which there was at any rate little or no recognition in the philosophy of the eighteenth century. The natural tendency, therefore, of that philosophy, everywhere but in England, was to seek the extinction of those institutions. In England it would doubtless have done the same, had it been strong enough: but as this was beyond its strength, an adjustment was come to between the rival powers. What neither party cared about, the *ends* of existing institutions, the work that was to be done by teachers and governors, was flung overboard. The wages of that work the teachers and governors did care about, and those wages were secured to them. The existing institutions in Church and State were to be preserved inviolate, in outward semblance at least, but were required to be, practically, as much a nullity as possible. The Church continued to 'rear her mitred front in courts and palaces,' but not as in the days of Hildebrand or Becket, as the champion of arts against arms, of the serf against the seigneur, peace against war, or spiritual principles and powers against the domination of animal force. Nor even (as in the days of Latimer and John Knox) as a body divinely commissioned to train the nation in a knowledge of God and obedience to his laws, whatever became of temporal principalities and powers, and whether this end might most effectually be compassed by their assistance or by trampling them under foot.

No; but the people of England liked old things, and nobody knew how the place might be filled which the doing away with so conspicuous an institution would leave vacant, and *quieta ne movere* was the favourite doctrine of those times; therefore, on condition of not making too much noise about religion, or taking it too much in earnest, the church was supported, even by philosophers—as a 'bulwark against fanaticism,' a sedative to the religious spirit, to prevent it from disturbing the harmony of society or the tranquillity of states. The clergy of the establishment thought they had a good bargain on these terms, and kept its conditions very faithfully.

The State, again, was no longer considered, according to the old ideal, as a concentration of the force of all the individuals of the nation in the hands of certain of its members, in order to the accomplishment of whatever could be best accomplished by systematic co-operation. It was found that the State was a bad judge of the wants of society; that it in reality cared very little for them; and when it attempted anything beyond that police against crime, and arbitration of disputes, which are indispensable to social existence, the private sinister interest of some class or individual was usually the prompter of its proceedings. The natural inference would have been that the constitution of the State was somehow not suited to the existing wants of society; having indeed descended, with scarcely any modifications that could be avoided, from a time when the most prominent exigencies of society were quite different. This conclusion, however, was shrunk from; and it required the peculiarities of very recent times, and the speculations of the Bentham school, to produce even any considerable tendency that

way. The existing Constitution, and all the arrangements of existing society, continued to be applauded as
the best possible. The celebrated theory of the three
powers was got up, which made the excellence of our
Constitution consist in doing less harm than would be
done by any other form of government. Government
altogether was regarded as a necessary evil, and was
required to hide itself, to make itself as little felt as
possible. The cry of the people was not 'help us', 'guide
us', 'do for us the things we cannot do, and instruct us,
that we may do well those which we can'—and truly
such requirements from such rulers would have been a
bitter jest: the cry was 'let us alone.' Power to decide
questions of *meum* and *tuum*, to protect society from
open violence, and from some of the most dangerous
modes of fraud, could not be withheld; these functions
the Government was left in possession of, and to these
it became the expectation of the public that it should
confine itself.

Such was the prevailing tone of English belief in
temporals; what was it in spirituals? Here too a similar
system of compromise had been at work. Those who
pushed their philosophical speculations to the denial
of the received religious belief, whether they went to
the extent of infidelity or only of heterodoxy, met with
little encouragement: neither religion itself, nor the
received forms of it, were at all shaken by the few
attacks which were made upon them from without.
The philosophy, however, of the time, made itself felt
as effectually in another fashion; it pushed its way *into*
religion. The *à priori* arguments for a God were first
dismissed. This was indeed inevitable. The internal
evidences of Christianity shared nearly the same fate;
if not absolutely thrown aside, they fell into the

background, and were little thought of. The doctrine of Locke, that we have no *innate* moral sense, perverted into the doctrine that we have no moral sense at all, made it appear that we had not any capacity of judging from the doctrine itself, whether it was worthy to have come from a righteous Being. In forgetfulness of the most solemn warnings of the Author of Christianity, as well as of the Apostle who was the main diffuser of it through the world, belief in his religion was left to stand upon miracles—a species of evidence which, according to the universal belief of the early Christians themselves, was by no means peculiar to true religion: and it is melancholy to see on what frail reeds able defenders of Christianity preferred to rest, rather than upon that better evidence which alone gave to their so-called evidences any value as a collateral confirmation. In the interpretation of Christianity, the palpablest *bibliolatry* prevailed: if (with Coleridge) we may so term that superstitious worship of particular texts, which persecuted Galileo, and, in our own day, anathematized the discoveries of geology. Men whose faith in Christianity rested on the literal infallibility of the sacred volume, shrank in terror from the idea that it could have been included in the scheme of Providence that the human opinions and mental habits of the particular writers should be allowed to mix with and colour their mode of conceiving and of narrating the divine transactions. Yet this slavery to the letter has not only raised every difficulty which envelopes the most unimportant passage in the Bible, into an objection to revelation, but has paralysed many a well-meant effort to bring Christianity home, as a consistent scheme, to human experience and capacities of apprehension; as if there was much of it which it was more prudent to leave *in nubibus*, lest, in the attempt to make the mind seize hold of it as a reality, some text might be found to stand in the way. It might have been expected that this idolatry of the words of Scripture would at least have saved its doctrines from being tampered with by human notions; but the contrary proved to be the effect; for the vague and sophistical mode of interpreting texts, which was necessary in order to reconcile what was manifestly irreconcilable, engendered a habit of playing fast and loose with Scripture, and finding in, or leaving out of it, whatever one pleased. Hence, while Christianity was, in theory and in intention, received and submitted to, with even 'prostration of the understanding' before it, much alacrity was in fact displayed in *accommodating* it to the received philosophy, and even to the popular notions of the time. To take only one example, but so signal a one as to be *instar omnium*. If there is any one requirement of Christianity less doubtful than another, it is that of being spiritually-minded; of loving and practising good from a pure love, simply because it is good. But one of the crotchets of the philosophy of the age was, that all virtue is self-interest; and accordingly, in the text-book adopted by the Church (in one of its universities) for instruction in moral philosophy, the reason for doing good is declared to be, that God is stronger than we are, and is able to damn us if we do not. This is no exaggeration of the sentiments of Paley, and hardly even of the crudity of his language.

Thus, on the whole, England had neither the benefits, such as they were, of the new ideas nor of the old. We were just sufficiently under the influences of each, to render the other powerless. We had a Government, which we respected too much to attempt to change it, but not enough to trust it with any power, or look to it for any services that were not compelled. We had a Church, which had ceased to fulfil the honest purposes of a church, but which we made a great point of keeping up as the pretence or *simulacrum* of one. We had a highly spiritual religion (which we were instructed to obey from selfish motives), and the most mechanical and worldly notions on every other subject; and we were so much afraid of being wanting in reverence to each particular syllable of the book which contained our religion, that we let its most important meanings slip through our fingers, and entertained the most grovelling conceptions of its spirit and general purposes. This was not a state of things which could recommend itself to any earnest mind. It was sure in no great length of time to call forth two sorts of men— the one demanding the extinction of the institutions and creeds which had hitherto existed; the other, that they be made a reality: the one pressing the new doctrines to their utmost consequences; the other reasserting the best meaning and purposes of the old. The first type attained its greatest height in Bentham; the last in Coleridge.

We hold that these two sorts of men, who seem to be, and believe themselves to be, enemies, are in reality allies. The powers they wield are opposite poles of one great force of progression. What was really hateful and contemptible was the state which preceded them, and which each, in its way, has been striving now for many years to improve. Each ought to hail with rejoicing the advent of the other. But most of all ought an enlightened Radical or Liberal to rejoice over such a Conservative as Coleridge. For such a Radical must know, that the Constitution and Church of England,

and the religious opinions and political maxims professed by their supporters, are not mere frauds, nor
sheer nonsense—have not been got up originally, and
all along maintained, for the sole purpose of picking
people's pockets; without aiming at, or being found
conducive to, any honest end during the whole process.
Nothing, of which this is a sufficient account, would
have lasted a tithe of five, eight, or ten centuries, in
the most improving period and (during much of that
period) the most improving nation in the world. These
things, we may depend upon it, were not always without much good in them, however little of it may now
be left: and Reformers ought to hail the man as a
brother Reformer who points out what this good is;
what it is which we have a right to expect from things
established—which they are bound to do for us, as
the justification of their being established: so that they
may be recalled to it and compelled to do it, or the
impossibility of their any longer doing it may be con-
clusively manifested. What is any case for reform good
for, until it has passed this test? What mode is there
of determining whether a thing is fit to exist, without
first considering what purposes it exists for, and
whether it be still capable of fulfilling them?

We have not room here to consider Coleridge's Conservative philosophy in all its aspects, or in relation to
all the quarters from which objections might be raised
against it. We shall consider it with relation to
Reformers, and especially to Benthamites. We would
assist them to determine whether they would have to
do with Conservative philosophers or with Conservative dunces; and whether, since there are Tories, it be
better that they should learn their Toryism from Lord
Eldon, or even Sir Robert Peel, or from Coleridge.

Take, for instance, Coleridge's view of the grounds of a Church Establishment. His mode of treating any institution is to investigate what he terms the Idea of it, or what in common parlance would be called the principle involved in it. The idea or principle of a national church, and of the Church of England in that character, is, according to him, the reservation of a portion of the land, or of a right to a portion of its produce, as a fund—for what purpose? For the worship of God? For the performance of religious ceremonies? No; for the advancement of knowledge, and the civilization and cultivation of the community. This fund he does not term Church-property, but 'the nationalty,' or national property. He considers it as destined for 'the support and maintenance of a permanent class or order, with the following duties. A certain smaller number were to remain at the fountain-heads of the humanities, in cultivating and enlarging the knowledge already possessed, and in watching over the interests of physical and moral science; being likewise the instructors of such as constituted, or were to constitute, the remaining more numerous classes of the order. The members of this latter and far more numerous body were to be distributed throughout the country, so as not to leave even the smallest integral part or division without a resident guide, guardian, and instructor; the objects and final intention of the whole order being these—to preserve the stores and to guard the treasures of past civilization, and thus to bind the present with the past; to perfect and add to the same, and thus to connect the present with the future; but especially to diffuse through the whole community, and to every native entitled to its laws and rights, that quantity and quality of knowledge which was indispensable both for the understanding of those rights, and for the performance of the duties correspondent; finally, to secure for the nation, if not a superiority over the neighbouring states, yet an equality at least, in that character of general civilization, which equally with, or rather more than, fleets, armies, and revenue, forms the ground of its defensive and offensive power.'

This organized body, set apart and endowed for the cultivation and diffusion of knowledge, is not, in Coleridge's view, necessarily a religious corporation. 'Religion may be an indispensable ally, but is not the essential constitutive end, of that national institute, which is unfortunately, at least improperly, styled the Church; a name which, in its best sense, is exclusively appropriate to the Church of Christ. . . . . The *clerisy* of the nation, or national church in its primary acceptation and original intention, comprehended the learned of all denominations, the sages and professors of the law and jurisprudence, of medicine and physiology, of music, of military and civil architecture, with the mathematical as the common organ of the preceding; in short, all the so-called liberal arts and sciences, the possession and application of which constitute the civilization of a country, as well as the theological. The last was, indeed, placed at the head of all; and of good right did it claim the precedence. But why? Because under the name of theology or divinity were contained the interpretation of languages, the conservation and tradition of past events, the momentous epochs and revolutions of the race and nation, the continuation of the records, logic, ethics, and the determination of ethical science, in application to the rights and duties of men in all their various relations, social and civil; and lastly, the

143

ground-knowledge, the *prima scientia*, as it was named, —philosophy, or the doctrine and discipline of ideas.

'Theology formed only a part of the objects, the theologians formed only a portion of the clerks or clergy, of the national Church. The theological order had precedency indeed, and deservedly; but not because its members were priests, whose office was to conciliate the invisible powers, and to superintend the interests that survive the grave; nor as being exclusively, or even principally, sacerdotal or templar, which, when it did occur, is to be considered as an accident of the age, a misgrowth of ignorance and oppression, a falsification of the constitutive principle, not a constituent part of the same. No; the theologians took the lead, because the science of theology was the root and the trunk of the knowledge of civilized man: because it gave unity and the circulating sap of life to all other sciences, by virtue of which alone they could be contemplated as forming collectively the living tree of knowledge. It had the precedency because, under the name theology, were comprised all the main aids, instruments, and materials of national education, the *nisus formativus* of the body politic, the shaping and informing spirit, which, educing or eliciting the latent man in all the natives of the soil, trains them up to be citizens of the country, free subjects of the realm. And, lastly, because to divinity belong those fundamental truths which are the common groundwork of our civil and our religious duties, not less indispensable to a right view of our temporal concerns than to a rational faith respecting our immortal well-being. Not without celestial observations can even terrestrial charts be accurately constructed.'—*Church and State*, chap. v.

The nationalty, or national property, according to

Coleridge, 'cannot rightfully, and without foul wrong to the nation never has been, alienated from its original purposes,' from the promotion of 'a continuing and progressive civilization,' to the benefit of individuals, or any public purpose of merely economical or material interest. But the State may withdraw the fund from its actual holders, for the better execution of its purposes. There is no sanctity attached to the means, but only to the ends. The fund is not dedicated to any particular scheme of religion, nor even to religion at all; religion has only to do with it in the character of an instrument of civilization, and in common with all the other instruments. 'I do not assert that the proceeds from the nationalty cannot be rightfully vested, except in what we now mean by clergymen and the established clergy. I have everywhere implied the contrary. . . . . In relation to the national church, Christianity, or the Church of Christ, is a blessed accident, a providential boon, a grace of God. . . . . As the olive tree is said in its growth to fertilize the surrounding soil, to invigorate the roots of the vines in its immediate neighbourhood, and to improve the strength and flavour of the wines; such is the relation of the Christian and the national Church. But as the olive is not the same plant with the vine, or with the elm or poplar (that is, the State) with which the vine is wedded; and as the vine, with its prop, may exist, though in less perfection, without the olive, or previously to its implantation; even so is Christianity, and *à fortiori* any particular scheme of theology derived, and supposed by its partisans to be deduced, from Christianity, no essential part of the being of the national Church, however conducive or even indispensable it may be to its well-being.'—chap. vi.

What would Sir Robert Inglis, or Sir Robert Peel, or Mr. Spooner say to such a doctrine as this? Will they thank Coleridge for this advocacy of Toryism? What would become of the three years' debates on the Appropriation Clause, which so disgraced this country before the face of Europe? Will the ends of practical Toryism be much served by a theory under which the Royal Society might claim a part of the Church property with as good right as the bench of bishops, if, by endowing that body like the French Institute, science could be better promoted? a theory by which the State, in the conscientious exercise of its judgment, having decided that the Church of England does not fulfil the object for which the nationalty was intended, might transfer its endowments to any other ecclesiastical body, or to any other body not ecclesiastical, which it deemed more competent to fulfil those objects; might establish any other sect, or all sects, or no sect at all, if it should deem that in the divided condition of religious opinion in this country, the State can no longer with advantage attempt the complete religious instruction of its people, but must for the present content itself with providing secular instruction, and such religious teaching, if any, as all can take part in; leaving each sect to apply to its own communion that which they all agree in considering as the keystone of the arch? We believe this to be the true state of affairs in Great Britain at the present time. We are far from thinking it other than a serious evil. We entirely acknowledge, that in any person fit to be a teacher, the view he takes of religion will be intimately connected with the view he will take of all the greatest things which he has to teach. Unless the same teachers who give instruction on those other subjects, are at liberty

to enter freely on religion, the scheme of education will
be, to a certain degree, fragmentary and incoherent.
But the State at present has only the option of such
an imperfect scheme, or of entrusting the whole business to perhaps the most unfit body for the exclusive
charge of it that could be found among persons of
any intellectual attainments, namely, the established
clergy as at present trained and composed. Such a
body would have no chance of being selected as the
exclusive administrators of the nationalty, on any
foundation but that of divine right; the ground avowedly taken by the only other school of Conservative
philosophy which is attempting to raise its head in this
country—that of the new Oxford theologians.

Coleridge's merit in this matter consists, as it seems
to us, in two things. First, that by setting in a clear
light what a national church establishment ought to
be, and what, by the very fact of its existence, it
must be held to pretend to be, he has pronounced the
severest satire upon what in fact it is. There is some
difference, truly, between Coleridge's church, in which
the schoolmaster forms the first step in the hierarchy,
'who, in due time, and under condition of a faithful
performance of his arduous duties, should succeed to
the pastorate,' and the Church of England such as we
now see. But to say the Church, and mean only the
clergy, 'constituted', according to Coleridge's conviction, 'the first and fundamental apostasy.'[1] He, and
the thoughts which have proceeded from him, have
done more than would have been effected in thrice the
time by Dissenters and Radicals, to make the Church
ashamed of the evil of her ways, and to determine
that movement of improvement from within, which

[1] 'Literary Remains,' iii. 386.

147

has begun where it ought to begin, at the Universities and among the younger clergy, and which, if this sect-ridden country is ever to be really taught, must proceed *pari passu* with the assault carried on from without.

Secondly, we honour Coleridge for having rescued from the discredit in which the corruptions of the English Church had involved everything connected with it, and for having vindicated against Bentham and Adam Smith and the whole eighteenth century, the principle of an endowed class, for the cultivation of learning, and for diffusing its results among the community. That such a class is likely to be behind, instead of before, the progress of knowledge, is an induction erroneously drawn from the peculiar circumstances of the last two centuries, and in contradiction to all the rest of modern history. If we have seen much of the abuses of endowments, we have not seen what this country might be made by a proper administration of them, as we trust we shall not see what it would be without them. On this subject we are entirely at one with Coleridge, and with the other great defender of endowed establishments, Dr. Chalmers; and we consider the definitive establishment of this fundamental principle, to be one of the permanent benefits which political science owes to the Conservative philosophers.

Coleridge's theory of the Constitution is not less worthy of notice than his theory of the Church. The Delolme and Blackstone doctrine, the balance of the three powers, he declares he never could elicit one ray of common sense from, no more than from the balance of trade.[1] There is, however, according to him, an Idea of the Constitution, of which he says—

[1] 'The Friend,' first collected edition (1818), vol. ii. p. 75.

'Because our whole history, from Alfred onwards, demonstrates the continued influence of such an idea, or ultimate aim, in the minds of our forefathers, in their characters and functions as public men, alike in what they resisted and what they claimed; in the institutions and forms of polity which they established, and with regard to those against which they more or less successfully contended; and because the result has been a progressive, though not always a direct or equable, advance in the gradual realization of the idea; and because it is actually, though (even because it is an idea) not adequately, represented in a correspondent scheme of means really existing; we speak, and have a right to speak, of the idea itself as actually existing, that is, as a principle existing in the only way in which a principle can exist—in the minds and consciences of the persons whose duties it prescribes, and whose rights it determines.'[1] This fundamental idea 'is at the same time the final criterion by which all particular frames of government must be tried: for here only can we find the great constructive principles of our representative system: those principles in the light of which it can alone be ascertained what are excrescences, symptoms of distemperature, and marks of degeneration, and what are native growths, or changes naturally attendant on the progressive development of the original germ, symptoms of immaturity, perhaps, but not of disease; or, at worst, modifications of the growth by the defective or faulty, but remediless or only gradually remediable, qualities of the soil and surrounding elements.'[2]

Of these principles he gives the following account:— 'It is the chief of many blessings derived from the

[1] 'Church and State,' p. 18.   [2] Ib. p. 19.

insular character and circumstances of our country, that our social institutions have formed themselves out of our proper needs and interests; that long and fierce as the birth-struggle and growing pains have been, the antagonist powers have been of our own system, and have been allowed to work out their final balance with less disturbance from external forces than was possible in the Continental States. . . Now, in every country of civilized men, or acknowledging the rights of property, and by means of determined boundaries and common laws united into one people or nation, the two antagonist powers or opposite interests of the State, under which all other State interests are comprised, are those of *permanence* and of *progression*.'

The interest of permanence, or the Conservative interest, he considers to be naturally connected with the land, and with landed property. This doctrine, false in our opinion as an universal principle, is true of England, and of all countries where landed property is accumulated in large masses.

'On the other hand,' he says, 'the progression of a State, in the arts and comforts of life, in the diffusion of the information and knowledge useful or necessary for all; in short, all advances in civilization, and the rights and privileges of citizens, are especially connected with, and derived from, the four classes,—the mercantile, the manufacturing, the distributive, and the professional.'[1] (We must omit the interesting historical illustrations of this maxim.) 'These four last-mentioned classes I will designate by the name of the Personal Interest, as the exponent of all moveable and personal possessions, including skill and acquired knowledge, the moral and intellectual stock in trade

[1] 'Church and State,' pp. 23–4.

rather of the principle, or the no-principle, on which it was supported. He saw in it (as we may surmise) the dangers of a change amounting almost to a revolution, without any real tendency to remove those defects in the machine, which alone could justify a change so extensive. And that this is nearly a true view of the matter, all parties seem to be now agreed. The Reform Bill was not calculated materially to improve the general composition of the Legislature. The good it has done, which is considerable, consists chiefly in this, that being so great a change, it has weakened the superstitious feeling against great changes. Any good, which is contrary to the selfish interest of the dominant class, is still only to be effected by a long and arduous struggle: but improvements, which threaten no powerful body in their social importance or in their pecuniary emoluments, are no longer resisted as they once were, because of their greatness —because of the very benefit which they promised. Witness the speedy passing of the Poor Law Amendment and the Penny Postage Acts.

Meanwhile, though Coleridge's theory is but a mere commencement, not amounting to the first lines of a political philosophy, has the age produced any other theory of government which can stand a comparison with it as to its first principles? Let us take, for example, the Benthamic theory. The principle of this may be said to be, that since the general interest is the object of government, a complete control over the government ought to be given to those whose interest is identical with the general interest. The authors and propounders of this theory were men of extraordinary intellectual powers, and the greater part of what they meant by it is true and important. But when considered as the foundation of a science, it would be difficult to find among theories proceeding from philosophers one less like a philosophical theory, or, in the works of analytical minds, anything more entirely unanalytical. What can a philosopher make of such complex notions as 'interest' and 'general interest,' without breaking them down into the elements of which they are composed? If by men's interest be meant what would appear such to a calculating bystander, judging what would be good for a man during his whole life, and making no account, or but little, of the gratification of his present passions, his pride, his envy, his vanity, his cupidity, his love of pleasure, his love of ease—it may be questioned whether, in this sense, the interest of an aristocracy, and still more that of a monarch, would not be as accordant with the general interest as that of either the middle or the poorer classes; and if men's interest, in this understanding of it, usually governed their conduct, absolute monarchy would probably be the best form of government. But since men usually do what they like, often being perfectly aware that it is not for their ultimate interest, still more often that it is not for the interest of their posterity; and when they do believe that the object they are seeking is permanently good for them, almost always overrating its value; it is necessary to consider, not who are they whose permanent interest, but who are they whose immediate interests and habitual feelings, are likely to be most in accordance with the end we seek to obtain. And as that end (the general good) is a very complex state of things, comprising as its component elements many requisites which are neither of one and the same nature, nor attainable by one and the same means—political philosophy must begin by a classification of these elements, in order to distinguish those of them which go naturally together (so that the provision made for one will suffice for the rest), from those which are ordinarily in a state of antagonism, or at least of separation, and require to be provided for apart. This preliminary classification being supposed, things would, in a perfect government, be so ordered, that corresponding to each of the great interests of society, there would be some branch or some integral part of the governing body, so constituted that it should not be merely deemed by philosophers, but actually and constantly deem itself, to have its strongest interests involved in the maintenance of that one of the ends of society which it is intended to be the guardian of. This, we say, is the thing to be aimed at, the type of perfection in a political constitution. Not that there is a possibility of making more than a limited approach to it in practice. A government must be composed out of the elements already existing in society, and the distribution of power in the constitution cannot vary much or long from the distribution of it in society itself. But wherever the circumstances of society allow any choice, wherever wisdom and contrivance are at all available, this, we conceive, is the principle of guidance; and whatever anywhere exists is imperfect and a failure, just so far as it recedes from this type.

Such a philosophy of government, we need hardly say, is in its infancy: the first step to it, the classification of the exigencies of society, has not been made. Bentham, in his 'Principles of Civil Law,' has given a specimen, very useful for many other purposes, but not available, nor intended to be so, for founding a theory of representation upon it. For that particular purpose we have seen nothing comparable as far as it goes, notwithstanding its manifest insufficiency, to Coleridge's division of the interests of society into the two antagonist interests of Permanence and Progression. The Continental philosophers have, by a different path, arrived at the same division; and this is about as far, probably, as the science of political institutions has yet reached.

In the details of Coleridge's political opinions there is much good, and much that is questionable, or worse. In political economy especially he writes like an arrant driveller, and it would have been well for his reputation had he never meddled with the subject.[1] But this department of knowledge can now take care of itself. On other points we meet with far-reaching remarks, and a tone of general feeling sufficient to make a Tory's hair stand on end. Thus, in the work from which we have most quoted, he calls the State policy of the last half-century 'a Cyclops with one eye, and that in the back of the head'—its measures 'either a series of anachronisms, or a truckling to events instead of the science that should command them.'[2] He styles the great Commonwealthsmen 'the stars of that narrow interspace of blue sky between the black clouds of the First and Second Charles's reigns.'[3] The 'Literary Remains' are full of disparaging remarks on many of the heroes of Toryism and Church-of-Englandism. He sees, for instance, no difference between Whitgift and Bancroft, and Bonner and Gardiner, except that the

[1] Yet even on this subject he has occasionally a just thought, happily expressed; as this: 'Instead of the position that all things find, it would be less equivocal and far more descriptive of the fact to say, that things are always finding their level; which might be taken as the paraphrase or ironical definition of a storm.'—'Second Lay Sermon,' p. 403.

[2] 'Church and State,' p. 69.   [3] Ib. p. 102.

last were the most consistent—that the former sinned against better knowledge;[1] and one of the most poignant of his writings is a character of Pitt, the very reverse of panegyrical.[2] As a specimen of his practical views, we have mentioned his recommendation that the parochial clergy should begin by being schoolmasters. He urges 'a different division and subdivision of the kingdom' instead of 'the present barbarism, which forms an obstacle to the improvement of the country of much greater magnitude than men are generally aware.'[3] But we must confine ourselves to instances in which he has helped to bring forward great principles, either implied in the old English opinions and institutions, or at least opposed to the new tendencies.

For example, he is at issue with the *let alone* doctrine, or the theory that governments can do no better than to do nothing; a doctrine generated by the manifest selfishness and incompetence of modern European governments, but of which, as a general theory, we may now be permitted to say, that one half of it is true and the other half false. All who are on a level with their age now readily admit that government ought not to *interdict* men from publishing their opinions, pursuing their employments, or buying and selling their goods, in whatever place or manner they deem the most advantageous. Beyond suppressing force and fraud, governments can seldom, without doing more harm than good, attempt to chain up the free agency of individuals. But does it follow from this that government cannot exercise a free agency of its

[1] 'Literary Remains,' ii. 388.
[2] Written in the Morning Post, and now (as we rejoice to see) reprinted in Mr. Gillman's biographical memoir.
[3] 'Literary Remains,' p. 56.

own?—that it cannot beneficially employ its powers, its means of information, and its pecuniary resources (so far surpassing those of any other association, or of any individual), in promoting the public welfare by a thousand means which individuals would never think of, would have no sufficient motives to attempt, or no sufficient powers to accomplish? To confine ourselves to one, and that a limited view of the subject: a State ought to be considered as a great benefit society, or mutual insurance company, for helping (under the necessary regulations for preventing abuse) that large proportion of its members who cannot help themselves.

'Let us suppose', says Coleridge, 'the negative ends of a State already attained, namely, its own safety by means of its own strength, and the protection of person and property for all its members; there will then remain its positive ends:—1. To make the means of subsistence more easy to each individual: 2. To secure to each of its members the hope of bettering his own condition or that of his children: 3. The development of those faculties which are essential to his humanity, that is, to his rational and moral being.'[1]

In regard to the two former ends, he of course does not mean that they can be accomplished merely by making laws to that effect; or that, according to the wild doctrines now afloat, it is the fault of the government if every one has not enough to eat and drink. But he means that government can do something directly, and very much indirectly, to promote even the physical comfort of the people; and that if, besides making a proper use of its own powers, it would exert itself to teach the people what is in theirs, indigence would soon disappear from the face of the earth.

[1] 'Second Lay Sermon,' p. 414.

Perhaps, however, the greatest service which Coleridge has rendered to politics in his capacity of a Conservative philosopher, though its fruits are mostly yet to come, is in reviving the idea of a *trust* inherent in landed property. The land, the gift of nature, the source of subsistence to all, and the foundation of everything that influences our physical well-being, cannot be considered a subject of *property*, in the same absolute sense in which men are deemed proprietors of that in which no one has any interest but themselves —that which they have actually called into existence by their own bodily exertion. As Coleridge points out, such a notion is altogether of modern growth.

> 'The very idea of individual or private property in our present acceptation of the term, and according to the current notion of the right to it, was originally confined to moveable things; and the more moveable, the more susceptible of the nature of property.'[1]

By the early institutions of Europe, property in land was a public function, created for certain public purposes, and held under condition of their fulfilment; and as such, we predict, under the modifications suited to modern society, it will again come to be considered. In this age, when everything is called in question, and when the foundation of private property itself needs to be argumentatively maintained against plausible and persuasive sophisms, one may easily see the danger of mixing up what is not really tenable with what is— and the impossibility of maintaining an absolute right in an individual to an unrestricted control, a *jus utendi et abutendi*, over an unlimited quantity of the mere raw material of the globe, to which every other person

[1] 'Second Lay Sermon,' p. 414.

could originally make out as good a natural title as himself. It will certainly not be much longer tolerated that agriculture should be carried on (as Coleridge expresses it) on the same principles as those of trade; 'that a gentleman should regard his estate as a merchant his cargo, or a shopkeeper his stock;'[1] that he should be allowed to deal with it as if it only existed to yield rent to him, not food to the numbers whose hands till it; and should have a right, and a right possessing all the sacredness of property, to turn them out by hundreds and make them perish on the high road, as has been done before now by Irish landlords. We believe it will soon be thought, that a mode of property in land which has brought things to this pass, has existed long enough.

We shall not be suspected (we hope) of recommending a general resumption of landed possessions, or the depriving any one, without compensation of anything which the law gives him. But we say that when the State allows any one to exercise ownership over more land than suffices to raise by his own labour his subsistence and that of his family, it confers on him power over other human beings—power affecting them in their most vital interests; and that no notion of private property can bar the right which the State inherently possesses, to require that the power which it has so given shall not be abused. We say, also, that, by giving this direct power over so large a portion of the community, indirect power is necessarily conferred over all the remaining portion; and this, too, it is the duty of the State to place under proper control. Further, the tenure of land, the various rights connected with it, and the system on which its cultivation is carried on,

[1] 'Second Lay Sermon,' p. 414.

are points of the utmost importance both to the economical and to the moral well-being of the whole community. And the State fails in one of its highest obligations, unless it takes these points under its particular superintendence; unless, to the full extent of its power, it takes means of providing that the manner in which land is held, the mode and degree of its division, and every other peculiarity which influences the mode of its cultivation, shall be the most favourable possible for making the best use of the land: for drawing the greatest benefit from its productive resources, for securing the happiest existence to those employed on it, and for setting the greatest number of hands free to employ their labour for the benefit of the community in other ways. We believe that these opinions will become, in no very long period, universal throughout Europe. And we gratefully bear testimony to the fact, that the first among us who has given the sanction of philosophy to so great a reform in the popular and current notions, is a Conservative philosopher.

Of Coleridge as a moral and religious philosopher (the character which he presents most prominently in his principal works), there is neither room, nor would it be expedient for us to speak more than generally. On both subjects, few men have ever combined so much earnestness with so catholic and unsectarian a spirit. 'We have imprisoned,' says he, 'our own conceptions by the lines which we have drawn in order to exclude the conceptions of others. *J'ai trouvé que la plupart des sectes ont raison dans une bonne partie de ce qu'elles avancent, mais non pas tant en ce qu'elles nient.*'[1] That almost all sects, both in philosophy and

[1] 'Biographia Literaria,' ed. 1817, vol. i. p. 249.

religion, are right in the positive part of their tenets, though commonly wrong in the negative, is a doctrine which he professes as strongly as the eclectic school in France. Almost all errors he holds to be 'truths misunderstood', 'half-truths taken as the whole', though not the less, but the more dangerous on that account.[1] Both the theory and practice of enlightened tolerance in matters of opinion, might be exhibited in extracts from his writings more copiously than in those of any other writer we know; though there are a few (and but a few) exceptions to his own practice of it. In the theory of ethics, he contends against the doctrine of general consequences, and holds that, *for man*, 'to obey the simple unconditional commandment of eschewing every act that implies a self-contradiction'—so to act as to 'be able, without involving any contradiction, to will that the maxim of thy conduct should be the law of all intelligent beings,—is the one universal and sufficient principle and guide of morality.'[2] Yet even a utilitarian can have little complaint to make of a philosopher who lays it down that 'the *outward* object of virtue' is 'the greatest producible sum of happiness of all men,' and that 'happiness in its proper sense is but the continuity and sum-total of the pleasure which is allotted or happens to a man.'[3]

But his greatest object was to bring into harmony Religion and Philosophy. He laboured incessantly to establish that 'the Christian faith—in which', says he, 'I include every article of belief and doctrine professed by the first reformers in common'—is not only divine truth, but also 'the perfection of Human Intelligence.'[4]

[1] 'Literary Remains,' jii. 145. [2] 'The Friend,' vol. i. pp. 256 and 340.
[3] 'Aids to Reflection,' pp. 37 and 39.
[4] Preface to the 'Aids to Reflection.'

All that Christianity has revealed, philosophy, according to him, can prove, though there is much which it could never have discovered; human reason, once strengthened by Christianity, can evolve all the Christian doctrines from its own sources.[1] Moreover, 'if infidelity is not to overspread England as well as France,'[2] the Scripture, and every passage of Scripture, must be submitted to this test; inasmuch as 'the compatibility of a document with the conclusions of self-evident reason, and with the laws of conscience, is a condition *à priori* of any evidence adequate to the proof of its having been revealed by God;' and this, he says, is no philosophical novelty, but a principle 'clearly laid down both by Moses and St. Paul.'[3] He thus goes quite as far as the Unitarians in making man's reason and moral feelings a test of revelation; but differs *toto cælo* from them in their rejection of its mysteries, which he regards as the highest philosophic truths, and says that 'the Christian to whom, after a long profession of Christianity, the mysteries remain as much mysteries as before, is in the same state as a schoolboy with regard to his arithmetic, to whom the *facit* at the end of the examples in his cyphering-book is the whole ground for his assuming that such and such figures amount to so and so.'

These opinions are not likely to be popular in the religious world, and Coleridge knew it: 'I quite calculate,'[4] said he once, 'on my being one day or other holden in worse repute by many Christians than the 'Unitarians' and even 'Infidels.' It must be undergone by every one who loves the truth for its own sake beyond all other things.' For our part, we are not bound

[1] 'Literary Remains,' vol. i. p. 388.   [2] Ib. iii. 263.
[3] Ib. p. 293.   [4] 'Table Talk,' 2nd ed. p. 91.

to defend him; and we must admit that, in his attempt to arrive at theology by way of philosophy, we see much straining, and most frequently, as it appears to us, total failure. The question, however, is not whether Coleridge's attempts are successful, but whether it is desirable or not that such attempts should be made. Whatever some religious people may think, philosophy will and must go on, ever seeking to understand whatever can be made understandable; and, whatever some philosophers may think, there is little prospect at present that philosophy will take the place of religion, or that any philosophy will be speedily received in this country, unless supposed not only to be consistent with, but even to yield collateral support to, Christianity. What is the use, then, of treating with contempt the idea of a religious philosophy? Religious philosophies are among the things to be looked for, and our main hope ought to be that they may be such as fulfil the conditions of a philosophy—the very foremost of which is, unrestricted freedom of thought. There is no philosophy possible where fear of consequences is a stronger principle than love of truth; where speculation is paralyzed, either by the belief that conclusions honestly arrived at will be punished by a just and good Being with eternal damnation, or by seeing in every text of Scripture a foregone conclusion, with which the results of inquiry must, at any expense of sophistry and self-deception, be made to quadrate.

From both these withering influences, that have so often made the acutest intellects exhibit specimens of obliquity and imbecility in their theological speculations which have made them the pity of subsequent generations, Coleridge's mind was perfectly free. Faith

—the faith which is placed among religious duties—
was, in his view, a state of the will and of the affections,
not of the understanding. Heresy, in 'the literal sense
and scriptural import of the word,' is, according to
him, 'wilful error, or belief originating in some per-
version of the will;' he says, therefore, that there may
be orthodox heretics, since indifference to truth may
as well be shown on the right side of the question as
on the wrong; and denounces, in strong language, the
contrary doctrine of the 'pseudo-Athanasius,' who
'interprets Catholic faith by belief,'[1] an act of the
understanding alone. The 'true Lutheran doctrine,' he
says, is, that 'neither will truth, as a mere conviction
of the understanding, save, nor error condemn. To love
truth sincerely is spiritually to have truth; and an error
becomes a personal error, not by its aberration from
logic or history, but so far as the causes of such error
are in the heart, or may be traced back to some antecedent unchristian wish or habit.'[2] 'The unmistakable
passions of a factionary and a schismatic, the ostenta-
tious display, the ambitious and dishonest arts of a
sect-founder, must be superinduced on the false doctrine before the heresy makes the man a heretic.'[3]

Against the other terror, so fatal to the unshackled
exercise of reason on the greatest questions, the view
which Coleridge took of the authority of the Scriptures
was a preservative. He drew the strongest distinction
between the inspiration which he owned in the various
writers, and an express dictation by the Almighty of
every word they wrote. 'The notion of the absolute
truth and divinity of every syllable of the text of the
books of the Old and New Testament as we have it,'
he again and again asserts to be unsupported by the

[1] 'Literary Remains,' iv. 193.   [2] Ib. iii. 159.   [3] Ib. p. 245.

Scripture itself; to be one of those superstitions in which 'there is a heart of unbelief;'[1] to be, 'if possible, still more extravagant' than the Papal infallibility; and declares that the very same arguments are used for both doctrines.[2] God, he believes, informed the minds of the writers with the truths he meant to reveal, and left the rest to their human faculties. He pleaded most earnestly, says his nephew and editor, for this liberty of criticism with respect to the Scriptures, as 'the only middle path of safety and peace between a godless disregard of the unique and transcendent character of the Bible, taken generally, and that scheme of interpretation, scarcely less adverse to the pure spirit of Christian wisdom, which wildly arrays our faith in opposition to our reason, and inculcates the sacrifice of the latter to the former; for he threw up his hands in dismay at the language of some of our modern divinity on this point, as if a faith not founded on insight were aught else than a specious name for wilful positiveness; as if the Father of Lights could require, or would accept, from the only one of his creatures whom he had endowed with reason, the sacrifice of fools! . . . Of the aweless doctrine that God might, if he had so pleased, have given to man a religion which to human intelligence should not be rational, and exacted his faith in it, Coleridge's whole middle and later life was one deep and solemn denial.'[3] He bewails 'bibliolatry' as the pervading error of modern Protestant divinity, and the great stumbling-block of Christianity, and exclaims,[4] 'O might I live

---

[1] 'Literary Remains,' iii. 229; see also pp. 254, 323, and many other passages in the 3rd and 4th volumes.
[2] 'Literary Remains,' ii. 385.
[3] Preface to the 3rd volume of the 'Literary Remains.'
[4] 'Literary Remains,' iv. 6.

but to utter all my meditations on this most concerning point . . . in what sense the Bible may be called the word of God, and how and under what conditions the unity of the Spirit is translucent through the letter, which, read as the letter merely, is the word of this and that pious, but fallible and imperfect, man.' It is known that he did live to write down these meditations; and speculations so important will one day, it is devoutly to be hoped, be given to the world.[1]

Theological discussion is beyond our province, and it is not for us, in this place, to judge these sentiments of Coleridge; but it is clear enough that they are not the sentiments of a bigot, or of one who is to be dreaded by Liberals, lest he should illiberalize the minds of the rising generation of Tories and High-Churchmen. We think the danger is rather lest they should find him vastly too liberal. And yet, now when the most orthodox divines, both in the Church and out of it, find it necessary to explain away the obvious sense of the whole first chapter of Genesis, or failing to do that, consent to disbelieve it provisionally, on the speculation that there may hereafter be discovered a sense in which it can be believed, one would think the time gone by for expecting to learn from the Bible what it never could have been intended to communicate, and to find in all its statements a literal truth neither necessary nor conducive to what the volume itself declares to be the ends of revelation. Such at least was Coleridge's opinion: and whatever influence such an opinion may have over Conservatives, it cannot do other than make them less bigots, and better philosophers.

[1] [This wish has, to a certain extent, been fulfilled by the publication of the series of letters on the Inspiration of the Scriptures, which bears the not very appropriate name of 'Confessions of an Inquiring Spirit.']

But we must close this long essay: long in itself, though short in its relation to its subject, and to the multitude of topics involved in it. We do not pretend to have given any sufficient account of Coleridge; but we hope we may have proved to some, not previously aware of it, that there is something both in him, and in the school to which he belongs, not unworthy of their better knowledge. We may have done something to show that a Tory philosopher cannot be wholly a Tory, but must often be a better Liberal than Liberals themselves; while he is the natural means of rescuing from oblivion truths which Tories have forgotten, and which the prevailing schools of Liberalism never knew.

And even if a Conservative philosophy were an absurdity, it is well calculated to drive out a hundred absurdities worse than itself. Let no one think that it is nothing, to accustom people to give a reason for their opinion, be the opinion ever so untenable, the reason ever so insufficient. A person accustomed to submit his fundamental tenets to the test of reason, will be more open to the dictates of reason on every other point. Not from him shall we have to apprehend the owl-like dread of light, the drudge-like aversion to change, which were the characteristics of the old un-reasoning race of bigots. A man accustomed to con-template the fair side of Toryism (the side that every attempt at a philosophy of it must bring to view), and to defend the existing system by the display of its capabilities as an engine of public good,—such a man, when he comes to administer the system, will be more anxious than another person to realize those capabili-ties, to bring the fact a little nearer to the specious theory. 'Lord, enlighten thou our enemies,' should be the prayer of every true Reformer; sharpen their wits,

give acuteness to their perceptions, and consecutive-
ness and clearness to their reasoning powers: we are in
danger from their folly, not from their wisdom; their
weakness is what fills us with apprehension, not their
strength.

For ourselves, we are not so blinded by our particular opinions as to be ignorant that in this and in
every other country of Europe, the great mass of the
owners of large property, and of all the classes
intimately connected with the owners of large property, are, and must be expected to be, in the main,
Conservative. To suppose that so mighty a body can
be without immense influence in the commonwealth,
or to lay plans for effecting great changes, either spiritual or temporal, in which they are left out of the
question, would be the height of absurdity. Let those
who desire such changes, ask themselves if they are
content that these classes should be, and remain, to a
man, banded against them; and what progress they
expect to make, or by what means, unless a process of
preparation shall be going on in the minds of these
very classes; not by the impracticable method of con-
verting them from Conservatives into Liberals, but
by their being led to adopt one liberal opinion after
another, as a part of Conservatism itself. The first step
to this, is to inspire them with the desire to systematize
and rationalize their own actual creed: and the feeblest
attempt to do this has an intrinsic value; far more,
then, one which has so much in it, both of moral goodness and true insight, as the philosophy of Coleridge.